SpringerBriefs in Economics

SpringerBriefs present concise summaries of cutting-edge research and practical applications across a wide spectrum of fields. Featuring compact volumes of 50 to 125 pages, the series covers a range of content from professional to academic. Typical topics might include:

- A timely report of state-of-the art analytical techniques
- A bridge between new research results, as published in journal articles, and a contextual literature review
- A snapshot of a hot or emerging topic
- An in-depth case study or clinical example
- A presentation of core concepts that students must understand in order to make independent contributions

SpringerBriefs in Economics showcase emerging theory, empirical research, and practical application in microeconomics, macroeconomics, economic policy, public finance, econometrics, regional science, and related fields, from a global author community.
Briefs are characterized by fast, global electronic dissemination, standard publishing contracts, standardized manuscript preparation and formatting guidelines, and expedited production schedules.

More information about this series at http://www.springer.com/series/8876

Mohamed A. Ramady

Financial Regulation and Liberation

Saudi Arabia's Path Towards True Global Partnership

Mohamed A. Ramady
London, UK

ISSN 2191-5504　　　　　　ISSN 2191-5512　(electronic)
SpringerBriefs in Economics
ISBN 978-3-030-68266-8　　　ISBN 978-3-030-68267-5　(eBook)
https://doi.org/10.1007/978-3-030-68267-5

© The Author(s), under exclusive license to Springer Nature Switzerland AG 2021
This work is subject to copyright. All rights are solely and exclusively licensed by the Publisher, whether the whole or part of the material is concerned, specifically the rights of translation, reprinting, reuse of illustrations, recitation, broadcasting, reproduction on microfilms or in any other physical way, and transmission or information storage and retrieval, electronic adaptation, computer software, or by similar or dissimilar methodology now known or hereafter developed.
The use of general descriptive names, registered names, trademarks, service marks, etc. in this publication does not imply, even in the absence of a specific statement, that such names are exempt from the relevant protective laws and regulations and therefore free for general use.
The publisher, the authors, and the editors are safe to assume that the advice and information in this book are believed to be true and accurate at the date of publication. Neither the publisher nor the authors or the editors give a warranty, expressed or implied, with respect to the material contained herein or for any errors or omissions that may have been made. The publisher remains neutral with regard to jurisdictional claims in published maps and institutional affiliations.

This Springer imprint is published by the registered company Springer Nature Switzerland AG
The registered company address is: Gewerbestrasse 11, 6330 Cham, Switzerland

*To my wife
Fatina
And to my grandchildren
Rayanne, Yara, Liyana, Asiya, Zakariya,
and Joseph,
who brought rays of sunshine and hope
during the dark days of the COVID 19
pandemic.*

Preface

Saudi Arabia has long been associated with its central role in the global energy market, with its decisions on production volumes affecting the global financial markets. However, the Kingdom has also emerged as a significant global financial player due to its large holdings of international currency, mostly US dollar reserves, and its dominance of the regional Gulf banking sector. But the path to financial regulation and liberation to unleash Saudi Arabia's potential has not come overnight but through incremental steps and learning by doing. The results speak for themselves as this book illustrates from the financial sector, with the book itself a concise version of *The Saudi Arabian Economy: Policies, Achievements and Challenges*, Springer 2010 Second Edition and bringing forward the story of the Saudi financial sectors development over the past decade and what a decade it has been. The Saudi Capital Market and evolution of its stock market—the *Tadawul*—are examined from an embryonic start in the 1970s to achieve a global emerging market status, the second largest after China, and home to the world's largest IPO—Saudi Aramco. The IPO of Saudi Aramco has attracted significant passive portfolio investment and spurred more liberalization of the Capital Market and the introduction of new financial products and instruments, such as listed REITs and both closed and open-ended funds and the establishment of the Saudi parallel stock market—*NOMU*—is examined as it opens up an avenue for SMEs to list and migrate to the main stock market. The CMA's regulations to open up to Qualified Foreign Investors is examined in depth, especially following the successful inclusion of the Saudi *Tadawul* in the key emerging market indices—the FTSE Russell, MSCI, and S&P Dow Jones EM indices. As noted above, all the above did not happen overnight. The Saudi Central Bank—SAMA—was established in 1952 and nearly died at birth due to a lack of supervision over the nascent banking sector, an absence of a national currency and acute government financial difficulties.

By 2020, SAMA had evolved into a global financial regulator overseeing not only local but international banks who once again are welcomed to operate following the period *of Saudization* of foreign banks operating in the Kingdom. The book examines in depth the centrality of the Saudi fixed currency regime to the US dollar, SAMA's monetary tools, macro-prudential policies and its supervision of the Saudi commercial banking sector and new sectors such as insurance, the emerging Fin Tech industry as well as a closer examination of SAMA's investment policies as custodian of the local currency. The growing levels of both domestic and international debt borrowings are examined as well as government policies to diversify the economy and reduce oil revenue dependency. The emerging role of the country's sovereign wealth fund—the Public Investment Fund—and the relationship between the two entities, given the PIF's large holding of Saudi bank stakes is closely examined, especially in the face of planned mega Saudi bank mergers and new Royal Act to transform SAMA to a Central Bank. The challenges faced by the Saudi regulators in the COVID 19 era are examined, along with the country's financial sector objectives as part of the Vision 2030 program, SME financing—a sector that has traditionally been ignored by the Saudi banks but is now a central plank in the country's Vision 2030 program, the growth of Fin Tech and digitization, the role of FDI in economic growth and the reasons behind Saudi Arabia languishing behind other countries in attracting FDI given the size of its economy, as well as Saudi Arabia's global role in assuming the presidency and hosting the 2020 G20 Summit, putting the Kingdom not only at the center of the global energy market, as a key proponent of the circular carbon economy but also an important global financial partner. It has been an incredible journey for a young country, and by all indications, the journey for expanded global partnership continues as Saudi Arabia also puts into practice its version of the circular carbon economy and being at the forefront of a new global digital economy.

London, UK   Mohamed A. Ramady
February 2021

Acknowledgements

With apologies to those inadvertently omitted, a word of thanks and appreciation is due to the following for their support and encouragement over the years in both a personal and professional basis: Dr. Abdelaziz Al Dukhayil, Dr. Majed Moneef, Khalid Al Zamil, Jamal Al Rammah, Ziyad Al Sudairy, Khalid Al Abdelkerim, Ahmed Banafe, Dr. Said Al Sheikh, Sadad Al Hussaini, Dr. Falih Al Sulaiman, Adib Al Zamil, Soliman Al Guwaiz, Kamal Lazaar, Omar Selim, Dr. Robert Walker, Dr. Abdelhaleem Mohaisen, Dr. Sara Vakhshouri, Junaid Akhtar, Dr. Halim Redhwi, Kevin Muehring, Mark Lawrence, Dr. Fadi Jardali, Dr. Bruce Davidson, Ibrahim Al Ankary, Prof. Tim Niblock, Christyan Malek, Dr. Sadiq Sohail, Dr. Abdelwahab Al Qahtani, Hamad Bin Sudd, Riyad Hammad, Dr. Khalid Al Binali, Ehtesham Shahid, Dr. Mohammed Al Sahlawi, Hatim Jamal, Tareq Mattar, Turki Al Subaei, Faisal Al Ankary, Nabil Diab, Munira Al Oudah, Wael Mahdi, Ruba Al Shehri, Mohammed Al Atawi, Nayef Al Watban, Waleed AbalKhail, Doug Leggate, Johanne Coatzee, Chris Kuplent, Karen Kostanian, Sassan Ghahramani, Charles Bell, Asit Sen, Charles Paxton, and Francisco Blanch.

My former students are heartily acknowledged for submitting valuable suggestions for inclusion in the book—Abdelkerim Marzook, Nayef Al Athel, Mohammed Al AlSheikh, Omar Al Oraifi, Turki Al Rammah, Abdelaziz Al Rammah, Majed Al Ahmad, and Ali Jasser. Finally, a special word of thanks is due to my Springer Editor, Lorraine Klimowich, and Franziska Sachsse for their tireless support in the Springer projects.

Contents

1 **Evolution of SAMA's Role and Monetary and Macro Prudential Policies** 1
   1.1 From Infancy to a Global Player 1
   1.2 SAMA's Governors and Their Challenges 3
   1.3 SAMA's Monetary and Macro-Prudential Policies 7
   1.4 The Centrality of a Pegged Currency Regime 11
   1.5 Managing the Country's Reserves: The Role of SAMA and the Public Investment Fund (PIF) 13
   1.6 The Rise of FinTech and New Banking Technology 16
   1.7 Regulating the Insurance Sector 17
   References 19

2 **The Saudi Banking Sector: From Saudization to Liberalization and Its Role in Economy Development** 21
   2.1 SAMA's Stewardship of the Banking Sector 21
   2.2 Evolution of the Saudi Banking System 22
   2.3 Saudi Banking Sector Performance 27
   2.4 Financing the SME Sector: Long Neglected But Now a National Priority 30
   2.5 The Growing Role of the Public Investment Fund 35
   2.6 Implications of Rising Sovereign Domestic and Foreign Currency Debt 37
   References 40

3 **The Saudi Capital Market: Coming of Age** 43
   3.1 Overview 43
   3.2 The Tadawul Stock Exchange: From a Humble Beginning to a Global Player 44
   3.3 Mobilizing Local and Foreign Investment: Developing an Advanced Capital Market 47
   3.4 The NOMU Parallel Market Adds Depth and Opportunity 51

	3.5	Growth of New Financial Products and Market Players-REIT's	53
	3.6	Strengthening the Mortgage Financial Legal Framework	55
	References		57
4	**Unfinished Business, Challenges Ahead and Conclusion**		**59**
	4.1	Overview	59
	4.2	FDI: Not Up to Expectations	61
	4.3	Vision 2030 Financial Plan: Adjustment in the Era of COVID 19	65
	4.4	GCC Monetary Union: Unfinished Business	68
	4.5	G20 Leadership: The Kingdom at Global Center Stage	70
	4.6	Conclusion	77
	References		82
Index			**85**

About the Author

Mohamed A. Ramady is a former Visiting Professor, Finance and Economics, at King Fahd University of Petroleum and Minerals (KFUPM), Dhahran, Saudi Arabia. He specializes on Saudi banking, OPEC, privatization, GCC regional energy, and geo-political risk assessment. He has authored many publications by Springer such as *"The Saudi Arabian Economy: Policies, Achievements and Challenges"*, Second Edition, 2010, as well as Editor of the *"GCC Economies: Stepping up to Future Challenges"*, 2012, and the *"Economic, Political and Financial Country Risk: An analysis of the GCC countries"* in 2013. In 2015, he published several books "OPEC *in a Shale Oil world—Where to Next?*" with Wael Mahdi, and Edited *"The Political Economy of WASTA—Use and Abuse of Social Capital Networking"*. In 2017, he published his latest book entitled *"Aramco 2030—Post IPO Challenges"*. Dr. Ramady was Project Manager to establish the guidelines for Saudi Arabia's WTO Centre for the Saudi Chambers of Commerce in 2012, as well-founding committee member to establish the *King Abdullah Science Park* at KFUPM and later the establishment of the *Dhahran Techno Valley* knowledge-based technology hub. He has held senior banking positions as Vice President with Citibank, where he was posted in Europe and the Middle East and seconded to the Saudi American Bank—SAMBA—and headed SAMBA's public sector as Senior SAMA Relationship Manager. He also served in executive positions with Chase Manhattan heading private banking to the MENA region, as well with First City Texas Bank; head of economics, investment, and planning with Qatar National Bank; and Advisor to the Chairman of Qatar International Islamic Bank.Dr. Ramady obtained his BA and PhD in Economics at the University of Leicester, UK, a Postgraduate master's degree in Economic Development, University of Glasgow, UK. He is a Fellow of the Chartered Institute of Bankers, UK.

Chapter 1
Evolution of SAMA's Role and Monetary and Macro Prudential Policies

A small leak can sink a great ship. Benjamin Franklin

Abstract The chapter examines SAMA's evolution of its role from establishment to date and its monetary and macro prudential policies, as well as the challenges faced by the different SAMA governors since its establishment in 1952 and Royal approval to transform SAMA to a Central Bank in 2020. The centrality of a fixed peg currency regime is examined and current SAMA oversight of Fintech, Cybersecurity and anti-money laundering programs. SAMA's role in managing the country's reserves and the role of the Public Investment Fund are examined, as well as SAMA's regulation of the growing insurance sector to ensure the growth of a Saudi insurance hub.

Keywords SAMA · Saudi Riyal · SAMA Governors · Fintech · Monetary and Macro-Prudential Policies · Fixed peg · PIF · Insurance

1.1 From Infancy to a Global Player

In order to better understand SAMA's current roles and responsibilities, one must also understand the historical trajectory of the institution in order to better appreciate the significant developments that have taken place in the Kingdom's financial history in comparison with other nations. It is easy to sometimes forget just how fast and how far the Kingdom has had to travel in a short period of time, celebrating its

90th anniversary in 2020, "learning by doing" along the way, and renamed as the Saudi Central Bank in November 2020, while retaining its SAMA acronym.

Compared to many western central banks, SAMA has had a more colorful and unorthodox history since its establishment in 1952 which has been well documented (Johany et al. 1986; Dukheil 1995; Banafa and Macleod 2017). When SAMA was established, the Kingdom did not have a monetary system of its own and foreign currencies circulated as a medium of exchange along with silver coins. There were no national Saudi banks, with banking conducted through foreign branches and specialized trading houses the most famous being the Netherlands Trading Company which later became the Saudi Hollandi (Dutch) Bank. The absence of a fixed exchange rate between the Silver riyal coins and foreign gold coins such as the "Maria Theresa" dollar, resulted in varied exchange rates.

SAMA's 1952 founding charter stipulated that it would conform to Islamic Law—it could not be a profit-making institution and could neither pay nor receive interest. There were additional prohibitions including one against extending credit to the government, but this was dropped in 1955 when the government needed funds and SAMA financed about one-half of the government debt that occurred in the late 1950s (Abdeen and Shook 1984; Banafa and Macleod 2017). This period saw SAMA almost dead at birth, as its formative years coincided with acute government financial difficulties due to runaway spending, and a depletion of reserves and the introduction of a paper riyal was abandoned at that time, but still assuming responsibility for maintaining the exchange rate of the Saudi Silver Riyal. The introduction of the Banking Control Law in 1966 was a watershed in SAMA's history as the new and overdue regulation clarified and strengthened SAMA's role in regulating the growing Saudi banking system (Jasser 2002). The new law vested SAMA with broad supervisory powers and allowed the agency to issue regulations, rules and guidelines regarding key international monetary supervisory developments that called for provision of capital adequacy, liquidity, reserve requirements and loan concentration ratios—something that is applicable today and are major SAMA regulatory tools as will be explored later. In essence, the new banking control law embedded the concept of a "universal banking model' that permitted banks to provide a broad range of financial services in traditional banking, investments and securities. From this base, SAMA saw its main role evolve as follows:

- *Issuing the national currency, the Saudi Riyal,*
- *Acting as a banker to the government and its agencies,*
- *Supervising commercial banks and exchange dealers operating in the Kingdom,*
- *Advising the government on the public debt,*
- *Managing the Kingdom's foreign exchange reserves,*
- *Conducting monetary policy for promoting price and exchange rate stability, and*

- *Promoting economic growth and ensuring the soundness of the Saudi financial system.*
- *Supervising cooperative insurance companies, finance companies and credit information companies.*

As will be noted later, over time SAMA has acquired for itself several other regulatory functions such as the supervision of the insurance sector, finance leasing, mortgage providers and any remaining money exchanges, as well as overseeing new developments in Fintech application. The Royal Approval for changing SAMA to a Central Bank on 24 November 2020, with direct reporting to the King, has been the latest significant change in SAMA's history to ensure that the new Central Bank which will continue to use the acronym "SAMA" due to its historical significance and relevance locally and internationally, will have the following objectives (SAMA 2020c), and aligns with SAMA's objectives listed earlier:

1. *Maintaining monetary stability,*
2. *Promoting stability of, and enhancing confidence in the financial sector,*
3. *Supporting economic growth.*

The current Central Bank Board of Governors is made up of serving and former SAMA officials (Governor Dr. Fahad Mubarak, Chairman, Ayman Al Sayari, Vice Chairman and Mr. Hamad Al Sayyari, former Governor), as well as private sector representatives (Mr. Khaled Al Juffali, and Mr. Abdulaziz Al Athel).

1.2 SAMA's Governors and Their Challenges

SAMA has been served by governors, some for short periods, others for extended periods with all facing challenges that tested the agency or offered new opportunities. All SAMA governors brought with them a blend of different management styles and professional backgrounds, mostly drawing upon western central bank and IMF philosophies, and this has been cemented by close technical and training cooperation carried out with leading western central banks which has resulted in SAMA adopting a basically western central bank approach in terms of bank supervision and risk management (Dukheil 1995; Banafa and Macleod 2017). This does not mean that SAMA does not have different policies from western central banks but that such differences can be explained by the environmental influences particular to a certain period of the Saudi economy, and the manner in which these particular environmental issues are handled which often determine the choice of policies that evolve.

Some of these environmental issues faced by SAMA were of an external global nature such as the Asian crisis of 1998, or the global financial crisis of 2008 with the collapse of Lehman Brothers in the USA, with capital markets all over the world going into meltdown and pressure on the dollar-riyal interest rate gap widening as Saudi banks were shut out of international funding putting pressure on the fixed peg. SAMA responded by placing dollar and riyal deposits with local banks. While the Saudi banking system weathered the international storm, spectacular corporate defaults nearer home put the banking system under strain again. The collapse of the Ahmad Hamad Al Gosaibi and Brothers (AHAB) and Maan Al Sanei, with around $22 billion in borrowings from Saudi and international banks in 2010 sent shock waves as most of the lending was done on 'name basis' and not backed by collateral. SAMA took prompt action but its powers to resolve the affair and protect the Saudi banks was limited and hampered by the absence of a bankruptcy code and legal power to collect money from debtors (Banafa and Macleod 2017). Companies such as AHAB and Al Sanei took advantage of regulatory arbitrage by locating operating units offshore and other tax havens, just as Lehman used different financing rules in London and New York to disguise its liabilities. This put central banks like SAMA in an unenviable position, as while informal arrangements and cooperation exists between regulators, the lack of formal arrangements creates loopholes. But lessons were learned and SAMA ensured that Saudi banks now pay closer attention to lending terms and financial standing of borrowers—basics of KYC—know your clients in banking.

The 1990–1991 Gulf crisis with Iraq's occupation of Kuwait was also a watershed moment for SAMA under Governor Hamad Al Sayyari who noted how the Kuwait Central Bank smuggled out key financial data through Saudi Arabia and then to London to effectively have a London based Kuwaiti commercial bank—the National Bank of Kuwait—act as the de factor Kuwait Central Bank (Prokesch 1990).

SAMA acted quickly and requested banks not to break time deposits to stop capital outflows and advised that they would support local banks and raised repo levels from 25% to 50% (Cooper 1990). To avoid a similar situation like Kuwait, SAMA ensured that the majority owned London based Saudi International Bank (SIB) had made preparations to also act as a de facto Saudi Central Bank (Al-Bawaba 1995).[1] The importance of having 'offsite' financial data in case of data loss/destruction was not lost and Saudi Arabia has been on the forefront in investing in advanced data centers using Cloud Technology (Paul 2017). SAMA now insists that Saudi banks download data on a daily basis in an offsite backup location. Table 1.1 below summarizes various SAMA governors' stewardship and the challenges they faced.

---

[1]The Author was a witness to these events when on 14 January 1991 he was present at the then Saudi Minister of Finance Mohammed Abal Khail's office in Riyadh, when Saudi International Bank's MD Mr. Peter de Roos was receiving last minute instructions before the launch of Operation Desert Storm on 17th January 1991.

1.2 SAMA's Governors and Their Challenges

Table 1.1 SAMA Governors 1952 to date

Governor and tenure	Key challenges faced and initiatives
1. George Blowers (USA) 1952–1954	• Issuance of first pilgrims receipts in 1953
2. Ralph Standish (USA) 1954–1958	• SAMA charter amended in 1957 emphasizing SAMA autonomy due to monetary and financial crisis in Saudi Arabia' • Board of Directors established
3. Anwar Ali (Pakistan) 1958–1974	• Institute of Banking established in Jeddah in 1965 • Foreign bank branches opened • Banking Control Law issued in 1966 • Riyad bank bailout
4. Abdulaziz Al Quraishi (Saudi Arabia) 1974–1983	• SAMA headquarters relocated to Riyadh • Ministerial Committee (Commerce, SAMA, Finance) to regulate stock market (1984) • Saudi company to register shares (1984) • *Saudization* of foreign banks started 1976 • Saudi Cairo bank problems leading to establishment of United Saudi Commercial Bank in 1997
5. Hamad Saud Al (Saudi Arabia) 1983–2009	• Committee for settlement of bank disputes (1987) • Fall in oil prices 1983 • Bankers Security Deposits Accounts (BSDA) introduced, precursor of govt. bonds and T-notes (1984) • Saudi Payment Network (SPAN) (1990) • 1990–1991 Gulf Iraq-Kuwait crisis /outward capital flows. SAMA support FX swaps, deposits • Saudi Arabian Riyal Interbank Express Electronic System _ SARIE (1997) • SAMA entrusted with licensing, controlling and supervising financial leasing companies (1999) • Cooperative Insurance Companies Control Law (2003) • Supervision of stock market moved to CMA (2004) • SADAD Payment System (2004)
6. Dr. Mohammed Al Jasser (Saudi Arabia) 2009–2011	• Managing the aftereffects of the 2008 global financial crisis • Pressure on Saudi Riyal peg • WTO accession 2005 • *Shariah* compliant banking opens (Al Inma, Al Bilad) • Saudi banks overseas branch opening • Development of Basel I Standards • Enhancing SAMA's training programs • Islamic Finance Supervision Division established
7. Dr. Fahad Al Mubarak (Saudi Arabia) 2011–2016	• Development of Basel II Standards • Initiating enhance macro-prudential supervisory methods • Anti-money laundering permanent committee set up. • Initiatives undertaken against financial and cyber risks

(continued)

Table 1.1 (continued)

Governor and tenure	Key challenges faced and initiatives
8. Dr. Ahmad Abdalkarim Al Kholifey (Saudi Arabia) 2016–2021	• Saudi Vision 2030 launched leading to FinTech Saudi initiative and Regulatory SANDBOX to assess impact of new technologies in financial services market, crypto currencies and digitalization of payments • Enhancing risk management and compliance regulations • Coordinating with Min. of Finance and CMA to implement initiatives under the Financial Sector Development Program • Comprehensive and specialized on-site bank inspection programs • Development of Basel III Standards • Streamlining the regulation of the Saudi Insurance sector • Saudi Real Estate refinancing Company commenced 2017 • G20 Finance Member • Change of SAMA status to a Central Bank
9. Dr. Fahad Al Mubarak (Saudi Arabia) 2021 to date	Saudi Bank Mergers

From Table 1.1, several items of significance stand out that will be ongoing regulation.

- *Cyber-Security Threats*: SAMA will continue to develop and mandate a cyber-security framework for the financial sector based on international best practices and continue to conduct specialized inspection programs of banking activities and operations, including information security and business continuity. Banks now immediately share critical cyber-security incidents/attempts with SAMA to ensure proactive measures are taken.
- *Role of FinTech*: SAMA has acknowledged the value added by financial services industry while appreciating the risks associated with Fintech innovation. The central bank has adopted a dual approach—the first is a risk-based approach to testing and regulating Fintech innovation—the 'regulatory Sandbox'—and launching the Future Banking Symposium consisting of different initiatives to support the development of the Fintech ecosystem in Saudi Arabia.
- *Anti-Money Laundering Regulations*: SAMA has developed a comprehensive set of revisions to both combating money laundering and combating terrorism and Terrorism Financing Laws, to be in line with the revised standards of the Financial Task Action Force and Saudi legal framework strengthened in customer due diligence framework, identification of beneficial owner, monitoring and reporting of suspicious activities and record-keeping. Over the past 2 years specialized AML/CFT Units have been established and reinforced at all supervisory authorities.
- *Financial Sector Development Program (FSDP)*: The FSDP is chaired by the Ministry of Finance, SAMA and the Capital Market Authority to monitor the economic health of the Kingdom and propose appropriate policy measures on subsidies, VAT and other monetary measures in line with changes in the macroeconomic environment, while maintaining financial stability.

1.3 SAMA's Monetary and Macro-Prudential Policies

SAMA has been making significant progress in establishing and formalizing a macro-prudential framework but admits that there is still room for improvement to fine-tune the macro-prudential 'tool kit' and close up some data gaps.

SAMA plays a vital role in the national economy through its monetary and financial stability and ensures credit availability to finance economic needs. One of the main responsibilities of monetary policy is the stability of the Saudi Riyal exchange rate in local and global markets where SAMA has maintained the stability of the exchange rate against the US dollar at 3.75 riyals per U.S. dollar since 1986, to be explored later below.

SAMA uses a range of monetary tools to achieve this goal, including repo and reverse repo rates, SAMA bills, reserve requirements, FX Swaps, direct deposits and other monetary tools available to manage liquidity (Jasser and Banafe 2003).

Figure 1.1 sets out SAMA's monetary policy framework, while Table 1.2 summarizes SAMA's monetary policy instruments and their comparative effectiveness.

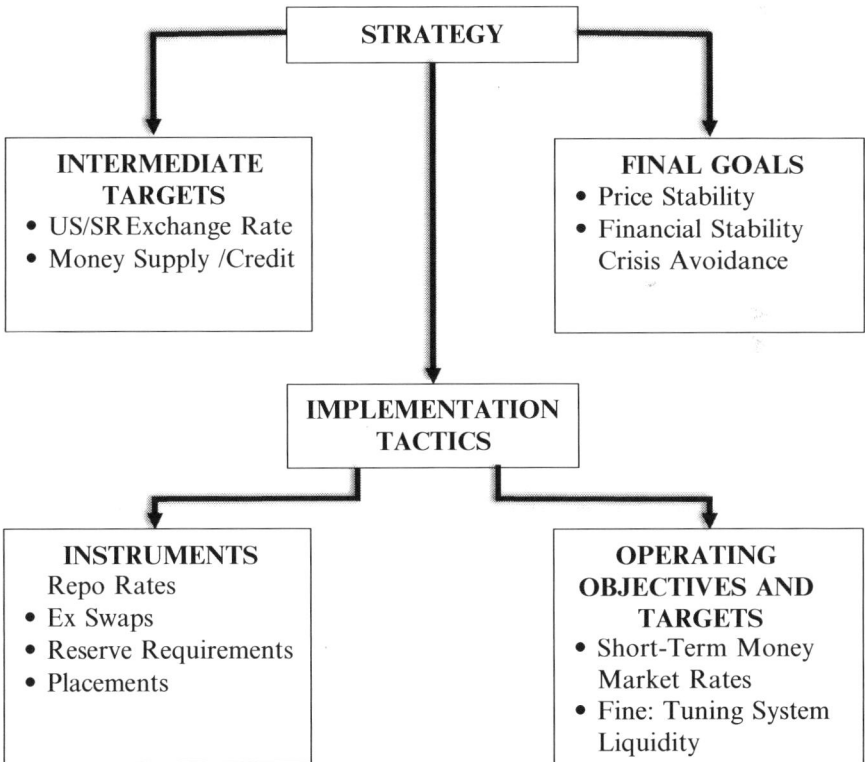

Fig. 1.1 SAMA's monetary policy framework

Table 1.2 SAMA' monetary policy instruments: comparative analysis

Policy instrument tool	Rationale and operational usage	Effectiveness
Cash reserve ratio (CRR)	• To ensure banks have adequate liquidity to cover customer deposits • Raised twice in April and May 2008 from 7 to 9% and then 13% for first time since 1980 on current account and from 2 to 4% on savings account • Reduced to 7% on current account in November 2008	• Used for implementing structural changes in bank liquidity (credit creation control) and for fine-tuning short-term liquidity • Produces strong signal effects but infrequently used • Not imposed on inter-bank transactions
Statutory liquidity ratio (SLR)	• Banks required to maintain minimum amount of specified liquid assets equal to 20% of demand and time deposits	• "Free liquidity" at disposal of banks is reduced and can influence overall bank lending structure (short/long term)
Repos	• SAMA alters liquidity position of banks by dealing directly in the market to make temporary additions to bank reserves through short-dated purchase agreements (overnight) • Set at 1% Aug. 2020	• Allows for short-term injection of reserves and automatic withdrawal upon repo maturity • Efficiency depends on SAMA's holding of securities and size and depth of market
Reverse repos	• Need for banks to place excess liquidity with SAMA through overnight matched sale-purchased operations • Reduced to 0.5% in Aug. 2020 from 2% in 2018	• SAMA can absorb rather than provide bank reserves • A definitive purchase of financial assets reversible at short notice not affecting prices in bond market; serves to regulate the money market
Foreign exchange swaps	• Intention to influence capital outflows, avoiding disruptions to monetary policy from foreign exchange markets • Used for liquidity management and currency speculation	• More flexible than repos/reverse repos in terms of their maturity and volume per deal • Affect liquidity but do not generally exercise influence on foreign exchange rate
Placement of public funds	• At SAMA's discretion to place governmental institutions' funds with selected banks	• A "rough tuning" instrument providing banks with long-term liquidity support • Can signal crisis management and problems in banks
Foreign exchange Intervention	• At SAMA's discretion in times of acute speculation	• Rarely used to stabilize spot and forward market in times of crisis

Source: SAMA, Annual Reports

Foreign exchange swaps are used to provide liquidity and absorb shocks stemming from the foreign exchange markets and are similar to repo transactions in securities, and SAMA has used swaps to provide foreign exchange liquidity when the Saudi Riyal has come under speculative pressures. This happened in 1993 and 1998 due to falling oil prices and in 2009 in the aftermath of the global financial crisis (Hamidy and Banafe 2013). More recently SAMA has used FX Swaps during the 2020 COVID-19 pandemic. Placement of public funds is a complementary instrument to the day-to-day liquidity management through repos, issuance of SAMA bills

1.3 SAMA's Monetary and Macro-Prudential Policies

and FX swaps. However, the use of placement of funds with banks could signal inherent crisis management and potential problems in banks (Ramady 2009).

During the last decade SAMA has used a number of macro prudential tools to smooth credit growth but before the 2008 global financial crisis central banks thought that the financial system was self-regulating because financial institutions had a vested interest in avoiding bad behavior and it was believed that a central bank's role was restricted to maintaining price stability and providing 'light touch' regulations (Banafa and Macleod 2017). The crisis demonstrated the inadequacy of this approach and showed that **micro-prudential** policy (looking at each bank individually) has to be matched by **macroprudential** policy (looking at the system as a whole). The new SAMA Central Bank Law of 2020 has confirmed that the Saudi Central Bank is responsible for setting the monetary policy and choosing its instruments and procedures (SAMA 2020c).

Since the experience of the global banking crisis of 2008, the objectives of macro-prudential policy are to limit systemic risk by focusing on the financial system as a whole with specific policy tools and guidelines. Just like other central banks, SAMA must choose the most appropriate macro-prudential measures for the Saudi financial system. SAMA, however, has to keep a close eye on other elements in the overall economy, the insurance sector and the domestic capital market besides banking sector key indicators. This is illustrated in Table 1.3 below.

Table 1.3 Internal SAMA Macro prudential dashboard

Indicator	Examples
Overall economy	Oil GDP Inflation Oil Prices
Credit overview	Credit growth (aggregate and by sector) Credit to GDP Credit Maturity
Banking Sector (Credit risk, funding and liquidity risk, capital adequacy, market risk, global risk, and interconnectedness)	Total assets Credit Revenues Profitability Expenses Nonperforming loans Loan to deposit Liquidity Capital adequacy ratio Investment breakdown
Insurance Sector (funding, liquidity risk, solvency, market risk)	Gross written premium Net loss ratio Profitability Expenses Liquidity Solvency Investment breakdown
Capital Market	Market capitalization Turnover Profitability Velocity

Source: Saudi Arabian Monetary Authority

According to the IMF, the macro prudential toolkit in Saudi Arabia is comparable to that of other commodity exporters although it has not been generally used in a countercyclical way (Arvai et al. 2014). The experience of other countries suggests that these policies have been effective in limiting systemic risk and that establishing a formal framework with SAMA as the designated macro prudential authority would bring clarity and credibility to macro prudential policy and ensure the willingness to act and coordinate with other Saudi authorities when necessary (Arvai et al. 2014). As noted in Table 1.3, SAMA shares this macro prudential policy with the Ministry of Finance and the Capital Market Authority (CMA).

However, SAMA does have, and exercised its regulatory *micro prudential* powers as applied to individual banks. These are set out in Table 1.4 below.

Table 1.4 SAMA macro prudential toolkit

Instrument	Regulatory requirement
Capital Adequacy Ratio	• Basel requirements of minimum 10.5% (including the conservation buffer)
Provisioning	• General: 1 % of total loans • Specific: Minimum 100% of NPLs
Leverage Ratio	• Deposits less than or equal to 15× Capital and Reserves
Cash Reserve Ratios	• 7% of Demand Deposits 4% of Time/Savings Deposits
Loan to value [LTV]	• Mortgage loans at or below 70% of residential real estate value
Debt Service to Income [DTI]	• Monthly repayments at or below 33% of employed salary and 25% of retired person
Statutory Liquidity Reserves	• Liquid assets not less than 20% of deposit liabilities
Liquidity Coverage Ratio [LCR]-Basel III	• 100% by 2019 [already fulfilled]
Net Stable Funding Ratio [NSFR]-Basel III	• 100% by 2019 [already fulfilled]
Counterparty Exposure	• Individual Exposure at or below 25% of bank capital (lowered to 15% by 2019)
Foreign Exposure	• SAMA approval needed before foreign lending [qualitative measure]

Note: The Basel III metrics, the Liquidity Coverage Ratio [LCR] and Net Stable Funding Ratio (NSFR) are designed to improve the liquidity of the banks and reduce the insolvency risk. Under the LCR, high quality liquid assets must be available to exceed the net cash outflows expected for the next 30 days. Similarly, the NSFR promotes banks' resiliency over a longer period. Banks resources must exceed their long-term commitments
Source: Banafa and Macleod (2017)

As part of its risk assessment toolkit, SAMA conducts micro stress testing of the Saudi banking sector on an annual basis to ensure the resilience of the sector to absorb macro-economic shocks and to identify weaknesses in the banking system as a whole or in individual banks to enable SAMA to design appropriate supervisory responses and pro-actively address such weaknesses. The lessons of the 2008 global financial crisis has been fully taken on board by SAMA, to ensure that Saudi banks can easily withstand various economic shock scenarios.

From Table 1.4, some key macro prudential toolkit measures are:

- *Loan to Value Ratio (LTV):* Since 2014 this has been used as an adjustable LTV ratio to prevent leveraged speculation on domestic property,
- *Debt service to income ratios:* Caps set on total consumer lending made by individual banks, to avoid consumer credit bubble,
- *Dynamic countercyclical loan loss provisions and Liquidity Coverage Ratio (LCR):* These are designed to improve the liquidity of the banks and reduce insolvency risk and build up their reserves when their profits are growing. SAMA has insisted that Saudi banks provisions against non-performing loans (NPL's) exceed 100%. Again, the lessons of the massive AHAB Gosaibi-Sanei defaults were taken on board.

1.4 The Centrality of a Pegged Currency Regime

Since the beginning of the post OPEC oil price hikes of 1973, Saudi Arabia's monetary and exchange rate policy has been dominated by a *de-facto* Saudi Riyal peg to either the Special Drawing Right (SDR) or the U.S. dollar. Prior to mid-1981 the riyal was loosely pegged with the IMF's SDR basket of currencies, but as noted earlier, since 1986 to the present time it has been tightly pegged with the U.S. dollar at SR3.75/$. Is this likely to change and what are the pros and cons of a fixed exchange rate that makes Saudi Arabia so embedded to the fixed rate regime, despite the fact that a fixed exchange rate policy raises a number of challenges, sometimes rendering Saudi monetary policy rather rigid (Ramady 2010; Banafa and Macleod 2017). Table 1.5 sets out the advantages and disadvantages of fixed and floating exchange rate regimes.

Table 1.5 Advantages and disadvantages of fixed and floating exchange rate regimes

Advantage	Disadvantages
Fixed exchange rate regimes	
• Maintains investors' confidence in the currency, thus encouraging domestic savings and investment and discouraging capital outflows • Reduces inflationary pressures associated with devaluation	• Does not allow the implementation of Independent monetary policy • Exchange rates cannot be used to adjust for external shocks or imbalances • A fixed peg is also a fixed target for speculators
Floating exchange rate regimes	
• Allows pursuit of an independent monetary policy; when an economy suffers a downturn, monetary expansion can soften the impact. Allows a country to adjust to external shocks through exchange rates; that is, lower export prices and that higher import prices would help the country regain external equilibrium	• Reduces investors' faith in the currency thus discouraging capital inflows to avoid exchange risk. • Floating rates can overshoot and become highly unstable, leading to speculation

Source: Adapted from Azzam (2002, p. 98)

While Saudi Arabia's current regime is a fixed conventional peg, the Kingdom's central bank is not statutorily committed to maintain the peg at that rate forever, and the peg can be adjusted either up or down when misalignment or intensive speculative pressure becomes a problem. As noted earlier, SAMA can and has defended the peg either through direct intervention in the spot and forward markets, or indirectly through monetary policy and domestic interest rates (such as a premium on Saudi riyal interest rates over the U.S. dollar). A key advantage of the fixed peg regime is stability, given that the peg is credible and provides a clear and easy-to-understand nominal anchor. Key disadvantages include requirement of a high level of international reserves and low ability to absorb shocks which are instead passed on to the real sector of the economy.

The fixed exchange rate policy of the Kingdom raises a number of challenges, sometimes rendering the monetary policy rather rigid. These occur during periods of intensive speculation on a possible revaluation or even a "de-peg" away from the dollar as during 2008. The SR peg to the U.S. dollar meant that SAMA had to reciprocate any Federal Reserve cuts to prevent arbitrage opportunities, the Saudi macroeconomic conditions unsupportive of any domestic cut, further strengthened the "de-peg" argument. This was made evident in SAMA repo rate cuts which ran contrary to appropriate policies when Saudi Arabia was witnessing record high inflation levels and rising liquidity, with the rate cuts leading to more severe negative real interest rates and fueled inflation further in 2008/2009 (Ramady 2010). SAMA however sees no permanent solution emerging from a revaluation of the currency and various SAMA governors have been vocal on record that the fixed peg is more of a benefit rather than a disadvantage. It was argued, correctly as it turned out by then SAMA Governor Al Jasser in 2009, that revaluation might temporarily reduce inflation, but the pressure might still be stocked up by domestic liquidity. As such, SAMA's policy credibility and the preservation of substantial reserves of liquid foreign currency assets are key parameters to maintaining the riyal peg to the dollar. On the former, SAMA Governor Al Kholifey (2016–2021) has been very explicit that over the years, SAMA has been able to maintain a stable exchange rate, even during different economic cycles and market conditions (SAMA Annual Report 2019), and that the short-lived volatility in both the spot and forward markets is evidence of the effectiveness of the current framework. The preservation of substantial reserves of liquidity to support the peg is one that is currently leading to market speculation for a revaluation or "de-peg" from the dollar, as also evidenced from the speculative attacks on the riyal in the 1990s when Saudi government reserves dipped to extremely low levels of SR 49.2 billion in 1998. At the end of 2015, these amounted to SR 2311 billion but have fallen back to SR 1700 billion in August 2020 (SAMA 2004, 2014). The fall in reserves over the period 2015–2020 has been triggered by a combination of sharply reduced oil prices, sluggish global energy demand since the 2020 COVID-19 pandemic and budget deficit drawdowns by the Kingdom. Some energy analysts are predicting that the depressed condition of oil prices and sluggish global economic recovery could last for longer periods, leading to concerns that more reserves could be exhausted unless government spending is curbed and new sources of revenues are obtained. However, such an analysis ignores the tremendous borrowing capacity of the Saudi government and its ability to borrow from both domestic and international sources, which will be explored later. This should allow for a comfortable level of foreign reserves are maintained to defend the fixed Saudi riyal peg, also underpinned by the Kingdom's Vision 2030 objective to gradually phase out Saudi Arabia's dependence on oil and rely more on other sources of income. In summary, there is little short or medium likelihood that SAMA will change the current fixed dollar peg rate policy, as there are also political considerations given close Saudi—U.S.A. economic and geo-political relationship. Another point that Saudi policy makers highlight, is that there is no such thing as a "painless devaluation" of the Saudi Riyal as a way to balance Saudi budget deficits by boosting government oil revenues which are denominated in Saudi riyals, as a devaluation would raise import costs to both the general public and the government.

1.5 Managing the Country's Reserves: The Role of SAMA and the Public Investment Fund (PIF)

Some questions have been raised about the roles of SAMA and the Public Investment Fund (PIF) in the future management of Saudi Arabia's reserves following the transfer of financial assets from SAMA to the PIF in 2016 of SR 100 billion, and in 2020 of $46 billion (Saudi Press Agency 2016; Bloomberg 2020). While the official statement in 2020 concerning the $40 billion transfer noted the 'exceptional ' nature of the transaction and that it was primarily driven by the PIF's mandate to implement its investment plans which includes seizing a set of investment opportunities that had arisen under the current global financial circumstances due to the COVID-19 pandemic, yet it is important to assess the different or overlapping investment strategies and philosophies of both SAMA and the PIF to conclude whether there is rivalry or complementarities in their investment strategies and whether the new Central Bank status changes these.

According to many analysts (Dukheil 1995; Banafa and Macleod 2017; Ramady 2010), SAMA sees itself as the custodian of the country's foreign exchange assets and has followed a relatively conservative approach with emphasis on liquidity of assets, credit quality, a diversified portfolio and risk-adjusted returns, while ensuring Saudi riyal exchange rate stability. The SAMA governor chairs the investment committee, which includes the Vice-Governor, Deputy Governor for Investments and technical experts. These meet on a quarterly basis to approve transactions for the following quarter but with the Deputy Governor for Investments reacting to short-term tactical movements due to external factors such as lower oil prices or movements in equity and bond prices. Figure 1.2 sets out SAMA's investment organization structure.

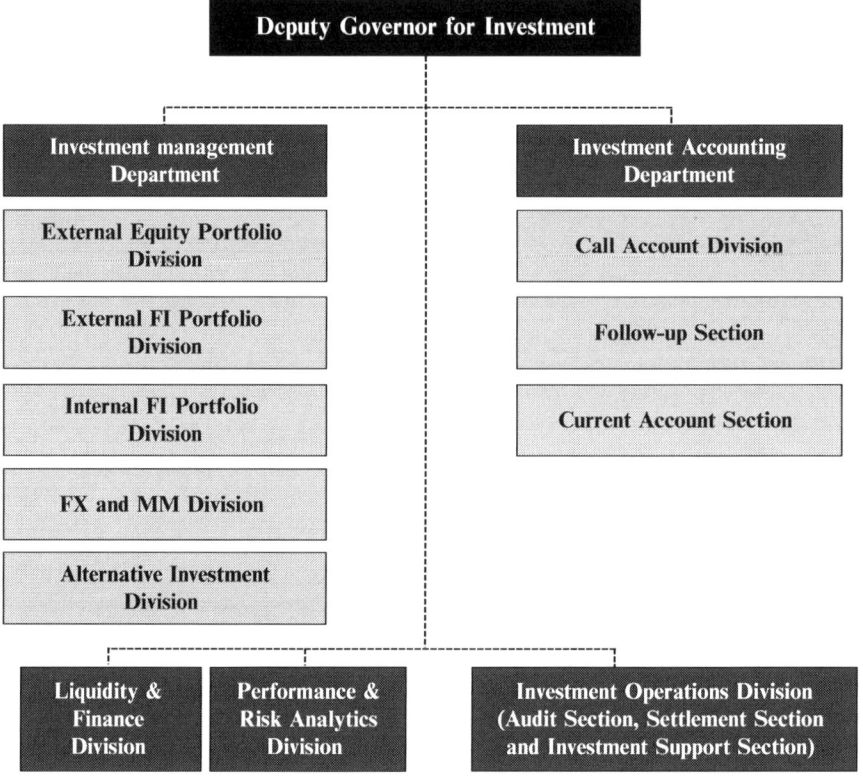

Source: Banafe, 2017

Fig. 1.2 SAMA's Investment process Organization Chart. Source: Banafa and Macleod (2017)

SAMA's investment decisions can be characterized as a 'top down' process starting with long-term macro analysis, foreign exchange and asset price forecasting, assessment of the investment matrix of expected returns, leading to SAMA's strategic asset allocation, and finally to a tactical asset allocation. Benchmarks for investments are selected on the basis of the monetary authority's risk tolerance for sovereign bonds and equities. The change in status to a Central Bank does not indicate that these practices will change.

Given the centrality of SAMA's fixed peg policy objective, SAMA has always divided its reserve portfolio into "liquidity" and "investment" segments, as the liquidity element is important to meet the needs of the Saudi banks for foreign-mostly U.S. dollar-exchange purchases at the pegged exchange rate. As such, priority is placed on liquid and quickly marketable international securities such as U.S. Treasury bills. SAMA also follows a rigorous and disciplined investment policy that is designed to ensure diversification to ensure a high risk-adjusted return on a range of asset classes to exploit investment opportunities in the face of changing global macro environment. However, the key objective remains backing of the

Saudi Riyal and meeting foreign remittance outflows, even if this means less returns on the portfolio. The primary asset allocation for the reserve portfolio is liquid money market instruments and highly liquid government bonds, while the main assets for the investment portfolio are medium to longer term growth assets, hedge assets and some real assets, but the last is small.

SAMA also makes deposits with foreign banks, and these are carried out according to the size of the recipient banks' equity capital and minimum credit rating of BBB minus, the lowest investment grade rating but usually higher. Such deposits are short term, usually up to 1 year. Investment in securities is much more selective and restricted to a few major economies sovereign and sovereign guaranteed agencies and other corporate obligations rated at a minimum of AA or AAA by Moody's, Standard and Poor's and Fitch, to minimize default risk.

While depending on its own internal management and technical investment expertise, SAMA also uses externally hired professional fund managers who can add value through their global research, expertise, track record and investment decision approach. Such external managers can be mandated to act either on an 'active' or 'passive' basis. While performance is an important element as to type of portfolio manager to choose, the fees charged are also an important consideration as 'active' portfolio managers fees are usually higher than those charged by 'passive' portfolio managers as the latter are sometimes both cost-effective and less time consuming and tend to perform well in mature markets with less economic and geo-political volatility, in contrast to emerging markets where 'active' portfolio management is better suited to assess these markets' growth potential and higher returns.

Besides traditional investment portfolios, SAMA also carries swaps and securities lending to restructure a portfolio's maturity or credit quality and improve liquidity, but rarely hedges its financial exposure through the use of derivative products. Similarly, gold has declined in importance for SAMA for backing the Saudi Riyal, with the local currency instead backed by a portfolio of reserve currencies. As of June 2020, SAMA's gold stock was SR 1624 billion ($433 million) showing a small increase over the years, standing at $233 million in 1994 and $219 million in 2002 (SAMA Annual Report 2003; Monthly Statistical Report 2020b).

It is not gold assets that are the main concern of SAMA, but the level of reserve assets and the rate of their depletion. Table 1.6 below summarizes these holdings over time.

Table 1.6 SAMA's international reserves 1963–2020 (SR billion)

Reserve	1963	1974	1987	1991	2005	2009	2015	2019	2020
• Foreign currency and bank deposits abroad	2.5	51.2	45.7	51.9	200.9	416.2	763.9	637.4	635.0
• Investment in foreign securities	0.12	25.9	171.3	102.6	369.9	1071	1501	1031	1020
Total	2.62	77.1	217.0	154.5	570.8	1487.2	2264.9	1668.4	1655

Source: SAMA Annual Reports, various Years, Monthly Statistical Report

What Table 1.6 illustrates is that SAMA's reserves have dramatically increased over the decades but that they have also been used as a buffer in times of global or regional crisis (1991), a built-up in times of higher oil prices (1974) and falls in periods of low oil prices (2019–2020). This forced the Saudi government and SAMA to adopt countercyclical policies to accumulate reserves to ensure a gradual transition and effective absorption of any shock, which aims to gradually phase out dependence on a major reserve volatility factor—dependence on oil revenues. This can be accomplished through several policy measures—cutting on public expenditure, raising domestic taxes and borrowing internationally. Each of these policy options comes with its own set of positive and negative consequences, discussed later.

1.6 The Rise of FinTech and New Banking Technology

According to SAMA, the Saudi central bank is one of the pioneers in the Gulf to experiment block chain technology for money transfers, with this one of the key innovative initiatives to enable and develop FinTech in the Kingdom. This has led to the Saudi FinTech Initiative in Cooperation with the CMA, the introduction of SAMA's Regulatory Sandbox noted earlier, and an array of digital banking services and payments. The Saudi central bank announced in April 2020 that it has permitted 9 FinTech companies as a new batch to operate in the Regulatory Sandbox, bringing the total number permitted by SAMA to 18.

In terms of activities, these Fintech companies can be classified according to the following type:

Number	Type
1	Financial Information Aggregation
5	Debt Crowd Funding Platforms
1	Consumabile Micro Lending
2	Digital Payments
3	Digital Savings Associations
1	Digital Savings Solutions
2	Buy Now – Pay Later

In January 2021, the Central Bank introduced 'open banking' that enables customers to securely share their data with third parties as a pivotal role in the future development of the financial sector (Saudi Central Bank, 2021).

SAMA's actions stems from its stated responsibilities to raise financial awareness among all community segments, support the development of the national economy, incentivize savings, financing and investments as part of the Financial Sector Development Program of the Vision 2030. The social effects of COVID-19, such as restricted mobility and the rise of remote working, has made the Kingdom's drive to develop a digital economy important, and SAMA has asked Saudi banks to encourage customers to carry out transactions using online or mobile banking. However, the amount of cash in circulation outside the banking sector has gone up since the pandemic outbreak in 2020, as some segments of society decided to hold more cash as a precautionary measure.

The Kingdom's digital transaction infrastructure is overseen by 'Saudi Payments', a wholly owned subsidiary of SAMA that is charged with ensuring that both banks and FinTech companies provide a secure payment system, including the launch of ESAL in 2019, a B2B invoicing platform designed to make the payment process more transparent and efficient. SAMA has licensed electronic wallet companies, and as of June 2020 there were local firms *STC Pay, Halalah, Gidig, Bayan Pay*, and a major global platform *Apple Pay*.

Saudi banks have seen the benefit of adopting financial technology—FinTech by initiating digital partnerships, with Riyad Bank, SABB and Al Rajhi banks taking the lead not only for individual clients but for the corporate banking sector such as SABB's SWIFT global payment initiative (gpi) to ensure that corporate clients conduct international payments at the same speed as domestic transactions with processing times reduced from days to hours. Saudi banks FinTech initiatives are also driven by the threat of foreign bank competition, from those that have recently entered the Saudi market as well as from regional banks, with the smaller Saudi banks facing the most pressure.

1.7 Regulating the Insurance Sector

In Dec. 2018, SAMA issued the FIB Rule for Licensing and Supervision of Foreign Insurance and re- insurance companies in the Kingdom to support local companies and create a Saudi insurance hub. Prior to FIB rules there were no provisions that allowed foreign insurance and reinsurance companies to open branches in Saudi and no limits on premium transfers from local branches to foreign branch of the company which now requires SAMA approval. The effect will be to retain premiums in the Kingdom and encourage local insurance/re insurance technical expertise (Barlow et al. 2020).

As part of Vision 2030, the Saudi insurance market has been going through a structural evaluation with the introduction of targeted regulations as noted above. Health insurance, in particular, has been a growing line of business in Saudi Arabia and has accelerated doing the 2020 COVID 19 pandemic. Gross written premiums in this sector have gone from SR 18.9 billion in 2015 to SR 22.5 billion in 2019 and by Q2 2020, this reached SR 12.9 billion out of total insurance gross written premium of SR 21.4 billion or 60% (SAMA, Monthly Statistical Report, Sept. 2020b). In November 2018, the Saudi Ministry of Health announced a new project to develop the health insurance industry in the Kingdom whereby the Ministry aims to provide 100% health insurance covers for Saudi nationals, both in the private and public sector, within the next 5 years.

The Saudi insurance market has been attractive to foreign insurance and re-insurance companies, especially the latter (Clyde & Co. 2015). On 17 December 2018, SAMA as the regulator for this sector, issued the Regulation "Rules for Licensing and Supervision of Branches of Foreign Insurance and/or Reinsurance Companies in Saudi Arabia (the FIB Rules).

Prior to the FIB Rules, there were no provisions that allowed foreign insurance and reinsurance companies to open branches in Saudi Arabia. Instead, insurers that wanted to provide services in Saudi Arabia had to set up a permanent establishment in order to do so. The FIB Rules imposed certain requirements, including confirmations from the company's home supervisory authority, hiring senior managers who must be resident in Saudi Arabia and submitting an extensive application that included a 5-year business plan, details of the insurance products to be sold and projected costs and underwriting growth (Barlow et al. 2020). Foreign Insurance Companies had previously preferred to operate their reinsurance business from offshore offices, especially Dubai, on the pretext that Saudi insurance professionals were not readily available, but SAMA seemed to address this by identifying suitably qualified Saudi nationals.

Following oil price volatility and regional economic and financial conditions where investment and capital reserves have been eroded forcing SAMA to introduce tougher rules regarding minimum capital reserves for insurance companies to ensure financial solvency and encouraged mergers and acquisitions, and has suspended several insurance companies from issuing new insurance contracts until they increase their capital and meet solvency requirements. The reason was obvious: given that Saudi Arabia's insurance market is largely fragmented with small companies competing against each other, the insurance sector needed further consolidation to create stronger companies capable of competing in the market, especially reinsurance which serves the mega Saudi Vision 2030, petrochemical and port expansion projects and which had attracted the offshore insurance sector to serve the lucrative Saudi market. In 2021, the Central Bank reiterated the need for Saudi insurance companies to look at further mergers and acquisitions to enhance the sector's capabilities (Argaam 2021).

As such, capital requirements for insurers are projected to increase from a minimum of SR 100 million to SR 500 million and capital requirements for reinsurers are projected to increase from a minimum of SR 200 million to SR 1 billion. To oversee the Saudi insurance sector, the following are the principal stakeholders: SAMA is the primary regulator of the insurance and reinsurance sector while health insurers are also supervised by the Council of Co-operative Health Insurance (CCHI). Insurers registered locally, which must also be publicly listed joint stock companies, are regulated by the Capital Market Authority—CMA and must also comply with the laws and regulations of the Ministry of Commerce and Investment (MOCI), the regulator for commercial companies. If a foreign shareholder is a partner in a Saudi insurance/reinsurance company like BUPA, they will be additionally required to obtain a foreign investment license from the Saudi Arabia General Investment Authority (SAGIA), and to abide by the Foreign Investment Act. Foreign ownership can be between 25% to 49% of a Saudi Insurance/reinsurance company. As such, the Saudi insurance sector is one of the more heavily regulated financial sectors in the Kingdom with close coordination between the above listed regulators.

All insurance and reinsurance companies must submit a tax and zakat declaration and audited financial statements. Non-Saudi Arabia residents' individuals and entities conducting business in the Kingdom under the Foreign Investment Act must declare annual dividends and pay 20% income tax on realized profits while the share payable by the Saudi Arabian investors is subject to a 2.5% zakat. There is a 5% withholding tax applicable on the repatriation of dividends by a foreign shareholder in a mixed foreign/Saudi entity. There is also a further withholding tax of 5% levied against any premiums paid to non-Saudi Arabia based insurance and reinsurance companies or commission paid to non-Saudi Arabia based brokers. The message is clear: Saudi based operations will have an advantage.

The Saudi focused regulatory changes and the size of the Saudi insurance market and its potential, especially in the health and motor insurance sectors, has witnessed Gross Written Premiums (GWP) rise from SR 8.58 billion in 2007 to SR 37.89 billion in 2019. Health accounted for 59% and Motor insurance 22.7% of the 2019 GWP premiums (SAMA 2020a, b, c).

References

Abdeen, A., & Shook, D. (1984). *The Saudi financial system in the context of Western and Islamic finance*. New York: John Wiley & Sons.

Al-Bawaba. (1995). *New boss for Saudi International Bank*. Retrieved October 9, 1995, from www.albawaba.com

Argaam. (2021). *Saudi Central Bank says M&A's in insurance sector to boost competition*. www.argaam.com.

Arvai, Z., Prasad, A., & Katayama, K. (2014). Macroprudential Policy in the GCC Countries. *IMF Staff Discussion Note SDN/14/01*, from https://www.imf.org/external/pubs/ft/sdn/2014/sdn1401.pdf

Azzam, H. (2002). *The Arab world: Facing the challenges of the new millennium*. London: IB Tauris.

Banafa, A., & Macleod, R. (2017). *The Saudi Arabian Monetary Agency 1952–2016: Central Bank of Oil*. London: Palgrave Macmillan.

Barlow, J., Alkhliwi, M., & Neighbour, T. (2020). *Insurance and reinsurance in Saudi Arabia: Overview*. Dubai: Holman Fenwick Willan Middle East LLP.

Bloomberg. (2020). PIF-Saudi transfers $40 billion to Wealth Fund. *Bloomberg*, Retrieved June 1.

Clyde & Co. (2015). *Insurance and reinsurance in Saudi Arabia: Overview*. Retrieved March 2015, from www.clydeco.com

Cooper, R. (1990). Under the gun: How they stopped the great Gulf panic. *Euromoney*, Retrieved September 1, 1990.

Dukheil, A. M. (1995). *The banking system and its performance in Saudi Arabia*. London, Saqi Books.

Hamidy, A., & Banafe, A. (2013). Foreign exchange intervention in Saudi Arabia. In *Market volatility and exchange rate interventions in EME's: What has changed?* (p. 73). BIS Papers.

Jasser, M. (2002). *Developing the financial sector for better economic growth*. Riyadh: SAMA. Future Vision of Saudi Arabia.

Jasser, M., & Banafe, A. (2003). *Monetary policy investments and procedures in Saudi Arabia*. Riyadh: SAMA.

Johany, A. D., Berne, M., & Mixon, W., Jr. (1986). *The Saudi Arabian economy*. Baltimore, MD: John Hopkins University Press.

Paul, K. (2017). *Exclusive: Apple and Amazon in talks to set up in Saudi services*. Retrieved December 28, 2017. Reuters. www.reuters.com

Prokesch, S. (1990). *Kuwaiti Bank serves an economy in exile*. New York Times, Retrieved September 12, 1990. www.nytimes.com

Ramady, M. A. (2009). Evolving banking regulation and supervision: A case study of the Saudi Arabian Monetary Agency (SAMA). *International Journal of Islamic and Middle East Finance and Management, 2*(3), 235–250.

Ramady, M. A. (2010). *The Saudi Arabian economy: Policies, achievements and challenges.* New York: Springer International.

SAMA. (2004). *A case study on globalization and the role of institution building in the financial sector in Saudi Arabia.* Riyadh: SAMA.

SAMA. (2003). *Annual report.* Riyadh: SAMA. from www.saam.gov.sa

SAMA. (2019). *Annual report*, Riyadh: SAMA. from www.sama.gov.sa

SAMA. (2014). *Annual report.* Riyadh: SAMA. from www.sama.gov.sa.

SAMA. (2020a). *Annual report.* Riyadh: SAMA. from www.sama.gov.sa.

SAMA. (2020b). *Monthly statistical report.* Retrieved September 2020, from www.sama.gov.sa

SAMA. (2020c). *King's Approval for the Saudi Central Bank Law and change of Name of the Saudi Arabian Monetary Authority.* Retrieved November 2020, from www.sama.gov.sa

Saudi Central Bank (2021). "Open Banking Policy". Saudi Central Bank, 18 January 2021. www.sama.gov.sa

Saudi Press Agency. (2016). Custodian of the two holy mosques directs to allocate SR 100 billion from Kingdom's reserves to PIF account. *Saudi Press Agency*, Retrieved November 30.

Chapter 2
The Saudi Banking Sector: From Saudization to Liberalization and Its Role in Economy Development

Money is a good servant but a bad master. Francis Bacon

Abstract SAMA's supervision of the Saudi banking sector is examined, as well as evolution of the Saudi banking sector in the period of globalization. The Saudi commercial banking sector's performance in supporting the Saudi economy is assessed including financing the neglected SME sector, as well as the growing role of the Public Investment Fund in the Saudi banking sector with planned mega Saudi bank mergers. The implication of a rising sovereign and domestic foreign currency debt is analyzed, along with options to control government expenditure under Vision 2030 constraints.

Keywords Banking Sector · SAMA Regulations · Bank Performance · SME's · PIF · Debt · COVID-19 effects

2.1 SAMA's Stewardship of the Banking Sector

In supervising the banking system, SAMA has adopted a generally conservative regulatory policy. This approach has its roots in the chaotic financial conditions of the early banking era of the 1950s and 1960s until the introduction of the Banking Law in 1966. Comparison with today's Saudi banking sector could not be different, as SAMA has strove to ensure an effective risk management and control structure supported by an institutional culture that ensures that Saudi banks have written policies and procedures that are actually translated into practice. SAMA has advocated that Saudi bank institution culture is determined and guided by the behavior of the banks' board of directors and senior management in ensuring ethical behavior, effective risk management and rigorous controls. Market discipline or lack of it can penalize banks that fail to manage their risks soundly, and SAMA has insisted that such market discipline must be supported by adequate transparent public disclosure and compliance with sound accounting standards to avoid state intervention to bail out or merge banks as noted earlier in the cases of Saudi Cairo and Riyad banks. Following such events SAMA has, as early as 1981, issued guidelines on power and responsibilities of the Board of Directors of Saudi Commercial Banks and has stressed the need to appoint qualified and independent board directors with experience, insight and force of character. SAMA has required banks in Saudi Arabia to meet the various corporate governance guidelines emanating from the Basle Committee on banking supervision. All Saudi banks now submit Basle compliance reports and their annual reports, with detailed accounting and risk assessment, a far cry from the 1960s, 1970s and early 1980s era bank annual reports bland assessments, pictures of dignitaries, office buildings and random ATM machines with happy clients. Even this state of affairs was much better than 1958, when SAMA noted in its First Annual Report of 1960, that 'no commercial bank submitted any statement of its financial position to the Monetary Agency' (SAMA 1960, p. 19).

The leadership role-played by SAMA over the past decades in promulgating sound corporate governance standards and culture has been reflected in the emergence of strong Saudi financial institutions and a credible banking system that is explored below. This has made the Saudi banks meet the challenges of liberalization and globalization more confidently, especially in the licensing of new foreign bank branches compared to the 1970s and 1980s period when SAMA pursued a policy of '*Saudization*' of foreign banks to shield domestic banks from foreign competition, as well as a policy tool to expand banking services to other parts of the country.

2.2 Evolution of the Saudi Banking System

Saudi Arabia is home to more than 27% of the GCC's total banking assets, the second largest banking industry in terms of assets and the largest in terms of market capitalization. Table 2.1 below sets out the evolution of the major events in the Saudi banking system, highlighting some of the major events such as bank insolvency, mergers, *Saudizaiton* of foreign banks and liberalization.

2.2 Evolution of the Saudi Banking System

Table 2.1 *Evolution* of the Saudi banking system (changes 1950–2020)

1950–60	• Establishment of SAMA • National Commercial Bank established
1960–70	• Merger of Al-Watany Bank into Riyad Bank due to technical insolvency • Introduction of Banking Control Law
1970–80	• Conversion of foreign bank branches into joint stock banks with Saudi participation completed • Post-conversion rapid growth in banking assets • Merger of branches of *Bank Melli Iran, National Bank of Pakistan and Banque de Liban et d'outre Mer* into United Saudi Commercial Bank, which then took over Saudi Cairo Bank
1980–90	• Increase in NPLs due to sharp decline in oil prices and economic stagnation • SAR peg to USD • Capital increase in existing banks • IT upgrade and introduction of ATMs
1990–2000	• Countercyclical fiscal policy via deficit financing • Rapid rise in banks' holdings of government debt • Bank restructuring and capital increases (merger of USCB into SAMBA)
2000–10	• Investment banking spun off from commercial banking into a separate entity • Licensing of additional foreign banks • Basel II implementation • Stock market collapse in February 2006 • Establishment of Saudi Credit Bureau • Domestic corporate credit event(Saad-AHAB) hitting banks' profitability
2010–20	• Enforcement of APR (Annual Percentage Rate) lending transparency • Encouragement of credit to SMEs • Issuance of SAMA bills for system liquidity management • Basel III implementation • NCB IPO • Changed name from Monetary Agency to Monetary Authority • Deposit Insurance fund • Vision 2020 and mega bank mergers • Deficit financing resumes • COVID-19 monetary measures

Source: Banafa and Macleod (2017)

By 1980 Saudi Arabia was home to 12 banks, 10 of which were partially foreign owned, and new entrants such as the Saudi investment bank in 1984 and the Al Rajhi Banking and Investment Corporation in 1988 and rising profitability (Essayyad et al. 2003). In the early 2000s an increasingly confident SAMA began to open the domestic market to majority foreign owned investment banks and commercial banks, a decision that overturned the 1975 requirement that all commercial banks be majority owned by a local partner—the beginning of the '*Saudization*' policy. There are many reasons given as to why this policy was initiated, but many agree that besides an element in protecting local banks from more powerful foreign competition, it was also the desire to see international best management banking practices and controls brought to the market from these foreign players, as well as expanding their presence to other parts of the country to service a booming economy once 'Saudized', as opposed to operating in one or two locations in either Jeddah or Riyadh (Dukheil 1995; Sheikh 1999; Suhaimi 2002; Ramady 2010).

As of the first quarter of 2020, Saudi Arabia's banking sector comprised 13 locally licensed banks, five of which held total assets worth more than SR 200 bn or $53.2 bn, with NCB the largest with assets of SR 507 bn and its position as a catalyst for domestic economic growth assured given a Saudi government majority stake in 1999 through the Public Investment Fund. The other mega Saudi banks are Al Rajhi (SR 384 bn), Riyad Bank (SR 265 bn), SAAB (SR 270 bn) following its merger with Alawwal Bank in 2019 (previously known of Saudi Hollandi Bank), and the fifth largest is SAMBA with total assets of SR 255 bn. SAMBA started its life as Citibank in Saudi Arabia and was notable for its introduction of the first ATM's electronic banking and payment cards as well as empowering generations of new Saudi banking management and executives through its own and Citibank training centers (Dukheil 1995; Wilson 1983).

The allure of globalization and domestic liberalization has been sweeping many global financial centers and noted by many observers of financial markets (Fayez 2002; Batlay and Sendan 2002; Knight 1998) including SAMA (SAMA 2004). The positive role that banks can contribute to economic growth has also been stressed if there is a deepening of local financial market players (Jasser 2002; Patrick 1996; Abdeen and Dale 1984). To meet these local and global regulatory responsibilities, the Saudi Arabian Monetary Agency changed its name to the Saudi Arabian Monetary **Authority** in 2016, keeping the acronym 'SAMA' in a move that has not attracted much attention (Argaam 2016). Supervision of banks would now take a higher role for the newly named 'Authority', and now as a Central Bank.

In the recent two decades SAMA's regulatory framework has undergone a series of changes designed to make it more attractive to foreign institutions and Vision 2030 has accelerated this trend. Currently, the Kingdom's banking industry has seen a new influx of foreign institutions with BNP Paribas and JP Morgan Chase the first market entrants under the revised framework. As of June 2020, 18 other regional and global financial institutions have joined them, attracted to the Kingdom's investment and commercial banking opportunities and capital market participation. Table 2.3 sets out the list of current domestic and foreign licensed banks and their status, as well as their Saudi branch network. While new foreign banks have been allowed, there were also some realignment of ownership in existing Saudi banks with the merger of Al Awwal Bank and SABB (Saudi British Bank) in 2019 and the sale by Credit Agricole of its final position in its stake in Banque Saudi Fransi in September 2020 to private investors (Argaam 2020a). Talks about a possible merger between Riyad Bank and NCB did not materialize in 2019 and both parties ended merger plans (Reuters 2019), but as discussed, NCB and SAMBA have signed a legally binding merger agreement in October 2020.

2.2 Evolution of the Saudi Banking System

Table 2.2 *Saudi* and foreign licensed banks and their branch network (Oct. 2020)

Bank name/ownership	Status	Branch network
(A) Saudi Banks		
1) NCB	Licensed	429
2) Saudi British Bank	Licensed—JV	112
3) Saudi Investment Bank	Licensed	52
4) Al Inma Bank	Licensed	98
5) Banque Saudi Fransi	Licensed	87
6) Riyad Bank	Licensed	275
7) SAMBA	Licensed	73
8) Al Rajhi Bank	Licensed	543
9) Arab National Bank	Licensed—JV	137
10) Bank Al Bilad	Licensed	111
11) Al Jazira Bank	Licensed	79
12) Gulf International Bank	Licensed	3
(B) Foreign Licensed		
1) Emirates NBD	Licensed	4
2) National Bank of Bahrain	Licensed	1
3) National Bank of Kuwait	Licensed	3
4) Muscat Bank	Licensed	1
5) Duetsche Bank	Licensed	1
6) BNP Paribas	Licensed	1
7) JP Morgan Chase	Licensed	1
8) Nat. Bank of Pakistan	Licensed	1
9) State Bank of India	Bank license cancelled	–
10) T.C. Ziraat Bankasi	Licensed	1
11) Ind. Comm. Bank of China	Licensed	1
12) Qatar Nat. Bank	Licensed	1
13) MUFG Bank	Licensed	1
14) First Bank Abu Dhabi	Licensed	3
15) Trade Bank of Iraq	Licensed—Not started yet	–
16) Standard Chartered	Licensed—Not started yet	–
17) Credit Suisse	Licensed—Not started yet	–
18) Bank of China	Licensed—Not started yet	–
Total branches		2019

Source: SAMA Quarterly Statistical Reports, August (2020a)

From Table 2.2 it becomes evident that the older established Saudi banks like NCB and Riyad Bank, and *Shariah* compliant banks like Al Rajhi, dominate the number of bank branches accounting for around 62% of total bank branches in 2020. The remaining *Saudized* joint venture banks—SABB and Arab National—account for 249 branches or around 13% of total branches. By contrast, foreign bank branches are 20 or a mere 1% of total branches with four banks licensed but still not started. Of the 20 foreign branches, the 3 GCC banks—Emirates NBD, National Bank of Kuwait and First Bank of Abu Dhabi account for 10 branches due to inter-GCC economic relations and GCC citizens using these branches to carry out financial and commercial transaction in the larger Saudi economy. Due to cost rationalization and more usage of ATM banking facilities, there has been a small reduction in bank branches in the Kingdom, to stand at 2019 in October 2020 from 2061 in August, with the reductions coming from Riyad Bank and Saudi British Bank (SAMA, Monthly Stat. Report, Oct. 2020a).

Although there are no Saudi banks with the world "Islamic" in their name, yet Islamic finance and *Shariah* compliant banking is very prominent as Table 2.3 below illustrates in terms of variety of *Shariah* compliant providers.

Table 2.3 *Shariah* compliant and conventional Saudi Banks

Bank name	Type			Ownership	
	SHARIAH	Conventional	Mixed	100% SAUDI	JV
1) AL INMA	√			√	
2) AL RAJHI	√			√	
3) AL BILAD	√			√	
4) JAZIRA	√			√	
5) NCB[a]			√	√	
6) RIYAD		√		√	
7) SAMBA[a]		√		√	
8) GIB		√		√	
9) SIB		√		√	
10) SAAB/AWWAL[b]		√			√
11) SAUDI FRANSI		√			√
12) ARAB NATIONAL		√			√

Source: Author review of Saudi bank annual reports designation
[a]In October 2020, NCB and SAMBA agreed on a merger
[b]In June 2019, Awwal Bank merged with Saudi British Bank (SABB)

Table 2.3 notes that there are only 4 fully *Shariah* compliant banks and one 'mixed' conventional/*Shariah* bank. These represent some of the largest Saudi banks (Rajhi, NCB). In terms of Islamic banking indicators for all the Saudi banks, there has been a perceptible rise in Islamic banking assets totaling SR 1.254 billion in 2017 to SR 1421 billion by Q1 2020 (SAMA Statistical Report, Sept. 2020a).

Besides foreign bank licenses, a further phase of market liberalization has taken place which allowed for expansion of foreign owned investment banks and financial houses which are licensed by the Capital Market Authority (CMA) rather than SAMA. Their activities will be assessed later in this chapter. These CMA licensed institutions numbered over 100 mid-2020 and include some of the world's largest investment banks including Union Bank of Switzerland, Credit Suisse, Goldman Sachs and Morgan Stanley.

2.3 Saudi Banking Sector Performance

The Saudi banking sector has faced a number of challenges in recent years, ranging from a decline in oil prices in the mid 1980s, the period after 2014 and the more recent COVID-19 economic impact, bringing to an end the double-digit growth that the sector had experienced for many years. This had ensured that Saudi banks capitalization and reserve buffers were built up to allow them to meet non-performing loan coverage as well as to support the government's domestic funding programs by purchasing bonds and SAMA Treasury bills.

For those that have worked in the Saudi banking sector, the state of the financial strength and size of the Saudi banks today compared to the earlier years is nothing but astonishing. Table 2.4 captures some of the changes in key indicators over these six decades. Some highlights are:

- *Customer deposit growth:* From less than SR 200 million in 1960, the Saudi Commercial Banks now boast a deposit base of SR 1865 billion ($497 billion) with current accounts still a major source of deposits, especially for the *Shariah* compliant banks like Al Rajhi, Al Inma and Al Bilad. In 2015, current account deposits accounted for nearly 61%, while in 2020 this had risen to 66%, due to the COVID-19 pandemic and higher demand for cash. This was also reflected in the rise in currency outside the banking system to 10.07% in 2020 from a steady level of 9.4% during the previous 5 years.
- *Lending:* Loans and advances to the private sector has risen dramatically to around SR 1.7 trillion in 2020 compared with a minimal SR 117 million in 1960, with lending taking off from 2009 onwards as banks showed a greater willingness to take on more risks following the 2008 global financial crisis. Lending to the private sector has tended to focus on the Saudi corporate market segment as the preferred route especially for the larger Saudi financial institutions and also of the new foreign banks entrants. The Saudi government has promoted lending to the Small and Medium Sized (SME) segment, and credit to this sector now accounts for around 6% in 2020 of total loan, a gain made from a low base. The government's stated objective to spur the growth of the SME sector has focused Saudi commercial bank minds and the growth in SME lending is expected to accelerate.

Table 2.4 Saudi banks key indicators 1960–2020 (SR bn)

Indicator/year	1960	1970	1980	1990	2000	2008	2015	2020
Total customer deposits	0.194	0.483	54.6	143.6	263.6	846.1	1617.1	1865
- Loans/advances to private sector	0.117	0.162	29.3	65.3	172.2	625.9	1384.0	1699
- Loans/advances to public sector	N/A	N/A	0.25	19.0	124.6	220.8	39.9	76.6
- Govt bonds holdings	N/A	N/A	N/A	49.3	100.2	128.3	86.1	429.3
- Total assets	0.215	0.584	93.62	232.0	453.2	1302.0	2233	2852
- Capital and reserves	0.143	0.167	0.848	17.36	43.5	128.9	270.4	380.1

Source: SAMA, Annual Reports (various), Monthly Statistical Report Aug. (2020a)
N/A not available

- *Capital and reserves:* Saudi banks are well capitalized, with a ratio of around 14% to total assets, far higher than the BIS minimum total capital ratio of 8% to risk-weighted assets. During the earlier periods, capital and reserves to total assets ranged from 66% in 1960 and 58% in 1970 as SAMA adopted a tough regulatory approach to ensure bank capital buffers are increased in face of the more turbulent earlier banking periods.
- *Government bonds:* Lending to the government became more prominent from the mid-1980s when oil prices fell sharply, as well as after 2015 when oil prices fell again. These trends are reflected in Table 2.3 with commercial bank bond holdings rising from 1990 to 2008 and falling back by 2015 when oil prices peaked at near $99 p.b in 2014. With oil prices remaining sluggish since 2015, the government has borrowed more from the Saudi banks to fund its budget deficit, a topic that will be addressed in more depth later in the chapter.

Drilling down by individual Saudi banks, Table 2.5 assesses various indices concerning loans, customer deposits, net income and their holding of government securities by year end 2019, while Table 2.6 highlights Saudi banks selected ratios over the period 2015–2020.

Table 2.5 Saudi banks economic activities: lending, government investments and net income (2019)

Bank name	Loans 2019 (SR bn)	Total customer deposits 2019 (SR BN)	Current L/D ratio (%)	Under/over L/D ratio (%)	Govt. T/bills security holding-2019	Net income 2019 (SR bn)
Riyad	174	195	89.2	(0.8)	132.4	11.48
NCB	282	353	79.9	(10.1)	55.9	5.60
SAMBA	141.6	180	78.7	(11.3)	24.9	10.16
Rajhi	249	299	83.3	(6.7)	2.9	0.31
Fransi	123.4	141.8	87.0	(3.0)	8.53	3.98
SAAB/Awwal	152.0	198.0	76.8	(13.2)	7.8	2.54
Al Bilad	59.3	66.8	88.8	(1.2)	7.6	3.11
ANB	117.8	130.9	89.9	(0.1)	15.9	2.84
Jazira	49.6	62.7	79.1	(10.9)	1.2	0.84
Inma	94.8	102.6	92.4	2.4	7.5	1.24
SIB	57.6	64.9	88.8	(1.2)	4.6	0.99
GIB	35.3	76.1	46.4	(43.6)	8.3	0.25
Total (SR bn)	1538.2	1870.8	82.2	(7.8)	277.5	43.34

Source: Saudi banks Q4 2020 financial statements

2.3 Saudi Banking Sector Performance

Table 2.5 highlights the relatively large concentration level of banking activity by a few banks—Riyad, NCB, Rajhi, SAMBA and Saudi British (SAAB). These five banks account for nearly 65% of total loans, 65% of total deposits, 80% of total government bills and securities, and 72% of net income. The recent merger between SABB and Awwal bank, and the planned mega merger between NCB and SAMBA will only accentuate the level of industry concentration by fewer banks with ramifications, explored later. What Table 2.5 also illustrates is that the smaller Saudi banks—Inma, Al Bilad—are at the SAMA mandated 90% loan/deposit ratio, but that there is still capacity for further lending by several of the larger banks which are below the 90% ratio, namely NCB, SAMBA and Rajhi Bank. This should provide some comfort to the Saudi government to call upon these banks to increase their lending, especially to the ongoing Vision 2030 mega projects as well as to the private sector. What is heartening though for borrowers, is that the Saudi Commercial banks are now extending credit on a longer-term basis as compared to their traditional preference for short-term (less than 1 year) loans which fell from 50% in 2015 to 42% in 2020, while longer term (over 3 years) rose to 43% in 2020 from 32% in 2015 (SAMA, Sept. 2020a, Statistical Report). Banks can do this if other indices underpin the state of their positive financial health, especially non-performing loans, capitalization and return on equity. This is illustrated in Table 2.6 below.

Table 2.6 Selected ratios of Saudi commercial banks (%)

Year	Capital and reserves to total assets	Regulatory capital to risk weighted assets	Tier 1 capital to risk weighted assets	Non-performing loans to total gross loans	Return on assets	Return on equity	Liquid assets to total assets
2015	16.72	18.1	16.2	1.2	2.0	14.5	17.5
2016	18.31	19.5	17.5	1.4	1.8	12.6	20.3
2017	19.41	20.4	18.3	1.6	2.0	12.9	21.6
2018	18.13	20.3	18.5	2.0	2.1	13.9	22.3
2019	19.10	19.4	18.1	1.9	1.8	11.9	25.4
Sept. 2020	19.98	19.1	17.7	2.3	1.0	6.7	25.2

Source: SAMA Monthly Statistical Report, Sept. (2020a)

The effects of the 2020 COVID 19 on Saudi banks is evident from some of the selected ratios in Table 2.6, specifically the rise in non-performing loans to total gross loans compared to earlier pre-COVID 19 periods, as well as a reduction in both return on assets and return on equity, but with capitalization ratios holding firm under SAMA's watchful eye on this critical bank ratio and the ability of Saudi banks to withstand further deterioration in their loan portfolio. This however saw credit provisions increase by 50% to SR 3.38 bn in 3Q 2020, compared with SR 2.25 bn in the same period 2019 (Argaam 2020b).

2.4 Financing the SME Sector: Long Neglected But Now a National Priority

Studies on the status and importance of the SME sector in Saudi Arabia have indicated that while SME's could, if they have the necessary financial support and government backing, make effective contribution to the local economy, in reality they have faced various internal and external constraints (Altokhais 2017; Waked 2016; Ramady 2010). According to empirical research (Rafiki 2019), some of the top crucial barriers facing Saudi SME's includes the following from respondents:

- *Problems in obtaining financial support*
- *Lack of credit options*
- *Inability to maintain proper business and accounting records,*
- *Inadequate business information*
- *Lack of business contacts,*
- *Lack of marketing knowledge*
- *Inability to employ skilled employees*

According to feedback from SME owners, accessing finance externally is considered a top priority to sustain business operations and at the same time to actively build relationships in a network among stakeholders. According to research (Altokhais 2017), it is not easy to motivate commercial banks to raise their lending levels to SME's due to perceived lack of SME transparency, poor credit information from credit registries and bureaus, and weak creditor rights (Ahmed 2012, Al Rashidi and Baakeel 2012). Lack of collateral, poor financial performance, infeasible business plans and incomplete information were also reasons of banks not lending (Waked 2016). To mitigate this, the Saudi government introduced the '*Kafala*' program for easier financial assistance to SME's in 2006, initially as a collaboration between the Ministry of Finance represented by the Saudi Industrial Development Fund (SIDF) and Saudi banks, with banks providing loans to SME's, about which 80% is guaranteed by the SIDF with an estimated SR 17 billion disbursed to 8500 SME beneficiaries over the period 2006 to 2016 (Altokhais 2017). By 2019, this program has been overtaken, with the *Kafalah* SME Financing Guarantee Program coming under the General Authority for Small and Medium Enterprises *(MONSHA'AT)*, which, according to SAMA, supported 3886 enterprises with total financing of SR 7.4 billion in 2019, compared with SR 4.9 billion and 3395 enterprises in 2018 (SAMA 2019, Annual Report). Support to the SME trade sector took the lion's share of funding followed by the construction sector as noted below in Table 2.7.

2.4 Financing the SME Sector: Long Neglected But Now a National Priority

Table 2.7 *Kafalah/Monsha'at* Funding by Sector (2019)

Sector	Beneficiaries (number)	Amount (SR billion)
• Trade	1634	2.9
• Building/ construction	1143	2.2
• Industrial Sector	322	0.701
• Tourism and Entertainment	286	0.552
• Financial and Business Sector	217	0.305
• Social and Personal Services	200	0.463
• Mining and Oil	2	0.002
• Agriculture and Fishing	12	0.028
• Electricity, Gas and Water	6	0.004

Source: SAMA (2020a)

Of interest is funding extended to the tourism and entertainment sector, given the emphasis placed on expanding this activity in line with Vision 2030 objectives to raising the level of SME's contribution to GDP from around 20% to 35% by 2030. In 2021, the Saudi cabinet took the logical step to boost the SME sector and approved the establishment of the SME's Bank to bring together all financing solutions under one umbrella (Arab News 2021). According to the Saudi government, there were around 950,000 SME's registered, providing one million Saudis with employment. However, the SME sector employs around 3.7 million foreigners mostly in the wholesale, retail, manufacturing and construction sector (Jadwa Investment 2019), although the number of foreign workers in these sectors has declined since the COVID 19 outbreak and slower economic growth with data for Q3 2020 real GDP contracting by 4.6 % year on year.

Since the launch of Vision 2030 in 2016, a series of reform measures have been rolled out by Saudi Arabia to support the SME sector after years of focusing on the larger economic sector and its projects. In December 2017, the government announced a SR 200 billion four-year program to stimulate private sector growth, with SR 40 billion expended in 2017 and SR 72 billion in 2018. The package provided four major initiatives for the SME's, as follows:

- Reimbursing government fees during the SME's first three operational years amounting to SR 7 billion,
- Indirect funding with SR 1.6 billion to provide different funding channels to investment institutions other than banks,
- Raising the capital of *Kafalah* by SR 800 million,
- A SR 2.8 billion venture capital fund targeting startups and SME investments, rising to SR 23 billion by 2020 through both private equity/venture capital.

Raising the contribution of SME's in the total economy is mentioned in several related Vision Realization Programs set out in Fig. 2.1 below.

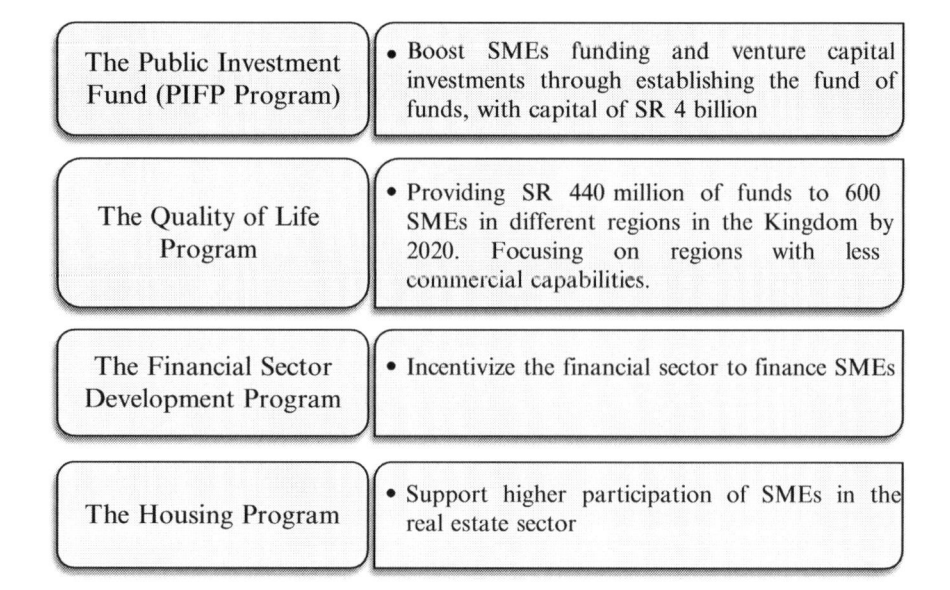

The Public Investment Fund (PIFP Program)	• Boost SMEs funding and venture capital investments through establishing the fund of funds, with capital of SR 4 billion
The Quality of Life Program	• Providing SR 440 million of funds to 600 SMEs in different regions in the Kingdom by 2020. Focusing on regions with less commercial capabilities.
The Financial Sector Development Program	• Incentivize the financial sector to finance SMEs
The Housing Program	• Support higher participation of SMEs in the real estate sector

Fig. 2.1 SME related Vision Realization Program

From Fig. 2.1, the key focus in the Vision on funding and enabling new financing solutions for SME's, is the PIF's indirect funding and venture capital initiatives with a capital of SR 4 billion. Another government initiative is the Saudi Capital Market Authority's launch of a 'parallel' market—*NOMU*—to help spawn some eligible and prosperous SME's to migrate to the main *Tadawul* stock market, to be explored in more detail in the next chapter. To help the SME's through this path, the Small and Medium Enterprises Authority (*MONSHA'AT*), introduced a separate *'Tomoh'* to provide support and business solutions on growth and market listing requirements. This will most probably initially target the 'medium' SME company profile as set out in *Monsha'a*t classification below (Table 2.8).

Table 2.8 *Monsha'a*t classifications for SME's

Micro	• Employee: 1–5
	• Revenue: up to SR 3 million
Small	• Employee: 6–49
	• Revenue: SR 3–SR 40 million
Medium	• Employee: 50–249
	• Revenue: SR 40–SR 200 million

2.4 Financing the SME Sector: Long Neglected But Now a National Priority

From this classification, SME enterprises are initially classified by revenue and in case revenue data is not available, then the number of employees classifies the SME enterprise. In order to overcome some of the barriers and obstacles faced by SME's noted earlier; the following initiatives were undertaken by different Saudi Ministries (Commerce, Economy Justice, Labor) to overcome perceived obstacles:

- Support SME's in accounting, zakat and taxation,
- Build a research center to provide accurate indicators and SME statistics,
- Design policies of SME's and facilitate the procedures of registration and promotion of innovation,
- Increase SME's in all regions of the Kingdom,
- Improve SME resources and productivity by training programs,
- Promote a '*Musharakah*' investment program to match investor funding 100% to SME contribution, to enable funding with a lower cost to SME's,
- Establishing a local rating agency for SME credit assessment.

Given the above multi-pronged initiatives and Vision 2030 support, according to latest SAMA data, financing the SME sector in the local financial sector—banks and finance companies—has risen from around 2% of total private sector loans in 2011, and surpassed the 2020 target of 5%, to reach 7.8% by Q2 2020. This is set out in Table 2.9 below.

Unsurprisingly, the bulk of credit facilities has gone to the 'medium' sized enterprises from banks, averaging around 74%, with 'micro' accounting for around 3%. Credit facilities provided by Saudi finance companies are less skewed, with medium enterprises receiving around 35% by Q2 2020, down from 42% in 2018. There could be many reasons for finance companies credit extension to the SME sector, namely a closer relationship and knowledge of SME owners and their plans, to taking higher risk in some opportunities rejected by traditional bankers.

Table 2.9 Credit facilities granted to micro, small and medium sized enterprises by Saudi Banks and Finance Companies 2018–2020

End of Period	Credit Facilities Provided by Banks					Credit Facilities Provided by Finance Company					Total Credit Facilities				
	Micro	Small	Medium	Total	% of Total Banks Credit Facilities	Micro	Small	Medium	Total	% of Total Banks Credit Facilities	Micro	Small	Medium	Total	% of Total Banks Credit Facilities
2018	3698	22,308	74,758	100,764	5.8	1207	3213	3335	7755	16.3	4905	25,521	75,093	108,519	6.0
2019	3526	23,008	81,437	107,971	5.7	1687	3810	3883	9381	19.0	5213	26,818	85,320	117,352	6.0
Q2 2020	5325	31,276	110,797	147,398	7.4	2069	4802	3856	10,728	21.1	7394	36,078	114,653	158,126	7.8

Source: SAMA Statistical Report Sept. (2020a)

2.5 The Growing Role of the Public Investment Fund

The Saudi Arabian government is committed to continue implementing its ambitious development and transformation programs under its Vision 2030 roadmap, as well as enhancing the role of the private sector. The PIF has emerged as a key policy instrument vehicle to improve domestic economic performance and to enhance the return on the Kingdom's investment assets. To do this, the government has transferred financial assets form SAMA's reserves to the PIF to implement its mandate (Saudi Press Agency 2016; Bloomberg 2020). Having a sovereign Wealth Fund (SWF) is not a new concept for some Gulf countries and the establishment of the Saudi PIF followed the model of three neighboring countries—Qatar, Kuwait and the UAE—which have financially empowered their SWF's for many years. From a bumble beginning in 1971, the Saudi PIF assets and investment portfolio has more than doubled since 2016 to well over $300 billion, with a sizeable portfolio in foreign assets along with a mandate that is very broad and intended to act both as a stabilization fund and a development fund. According to the PIF, it is intended to diversify governmental revenues, open up new private sector opportunities at home, channel foreign direct investment to Saudi Arabia and facilitate knowledge and technology transfer to the Kingdom (Roll 2019). All this implies that the PIF will continue to have access to a substantial part of Saudi public finances through the budget and from reserve transfers by SAMA to sustain the PIF as the pre-eminent "engine of growth" (Kingdom of Saudi Arabia 2017).

To meet its objectives, the PIF no longer functions as a passive financing partner and lender but acts much more proactively to seek out domestic and international opportunities to become a global investment powerhouse (Gamal El Din and Nereim 2020). According to those that track its investments, in 2020 alone, the PIF has bought over $8.2 billion worth of new investments in global stocks in companies and industries which have been negatively affected by the market crash in their stock prices due to the Coronavirus pandemic, with investments ranging from energy companies (BP, Royal Dutch Shell, Suncor Energy, Total, Equinor), to travel, tourism and entertainment (Boeing, Marriott, Carnival, Live Nation Entertainment), and also in banks and IT sectors (Forbes 2020). This follows on from the high profile PIF investments through the Japanese owned Softbank Fund (Torchia et al. 2018). While the PIF's investments and acquisitions make the headlines, such as those made in Uber, Tesla, Lucid Motors, Six Flags, others note that compared to SAMA's structured investment management process and oversight, the PIF's institutional structure and authority is more opaque and that while several key Saudi Ministers sit on the Board of Directors of the PIF, SAMA is no longer represented on the PIF's Board of Directors (Roll 2019).

The PIF's program states that the SWF should grow to $400 billion by 2020 (Kingdom of Saudi Arabia 2017). In a further sign of its growing importance, the Saudi *Shoura* consultative council approved amendments in 2018 that largely guarantees the PIF's financial and administrative independence (Anderson, 2018). While it can be argued that the functions of both SAMA and the PIF are clearly set out—the former on maintaining the national reserves in a prudent manner to support the fixed peg policy—the latter on maximizing non-oil income investments by taking marketing risk, the change of name of SAMA from an 'Agency' to 'Authority' seems to imply that SAMA will focus in the future more as guardian of the national currency and overseeing the expanded financial sector as noted earlier in the chapter. This has been superseded again. The change by the Saudi *Shourah* council in the status of SAMA to become a Central Bank through a new Saudi Central Bank Law was granted Royal Approval on 24 November 2020 while allowing the Saudi Central Bank to still use its SAMA acronym, granting a rebranded SAMA more independence and flexibility in its investment function. This could change the dynamics between it and the PIF, but it is too early to assess what this change in status to a Central Bank will entail (Saudi Press Agency 2020; SAMA 2020b), although the new Law has allowed the Central Bank to buy and own real estate if the purpose was to diversify its foreign investments (Saudi Gazette 2020). Furthermore the Saudi Central Bank updated its mandate to include supporting economic growth as one of its operating primary objectives and formally changing its operating principles for the first time in more than 60 years from those noted earlier in the chapter (Martin and Abu Omar 2020). This has not stopped some commentators to state that the new Central Bank designation could diminish its role of investing Saudi Arabia's hard currency surpluses in favour of the sovereign wealth fund PIF and underscores a radical shift from being a conservative investor to a more aggressive and higher risk investment approach (England and Kerr 2021). To allay such fears, the Saudi Finance Minister Al Jadaan was quoted as saying that the new adjustments to the Saudi Central Bank will not affect its core obligations including sustaining adequate reserves to protect the riyal-dollar peg and its monetary stability, and that the change in name was to bring the regulator into line with worldwide requirements and supply it with larger independence and empower the Central Bank to issuing bank licenses which had been dealt with by the Ministry of Finance, and that the Kingdom had a clear proposal of how the surpluses are distributed between SAMA and the PIF and that the PIF had adequate funding and would get extra funding from privatization and any additional itemizing of Saudi Aramco share sales (Argaam 2021). Meanwhile, the PIF continues to have the political support of Saudi leadership, especially the PIF's investment programs. In November 2020, the Saudi Crown Prince announced that the PIF will inject SR 150 billion ($40 billion) annually in the economy in 2021 and 2022 and target local investments, and that the fund managed to create a higher returns on investments at a minimum of 7% from 2% since its establishment, with some investments exceeding 70% and others making more than 140m%, and that the PIF has become one of the " key drivers" for the Saudi economy, doubling its size from SR 560 billion to more than SR 1.3 trillion (Arab News 2020a). In 2021, Crown Prince Mohammed bin Salman launched a new five year strategy for the PIFV to create 1.8 million jobs by 2025 and that the PIF created 10 new sectors and generated 331,000 direct and indirect jobs to date (Radwan 2021).

While cooperation between the two institutions is vital to meeting the economic objectives of the Kingdom, there is significant PIF ownership of Saudi banks shareholding, such as in NCB, SAMBA, Riyad Bank and Al Inma Bank, which together account for around 45% of total Saudi banking financial assets. This is illustrated in Fig. 2.2 below.

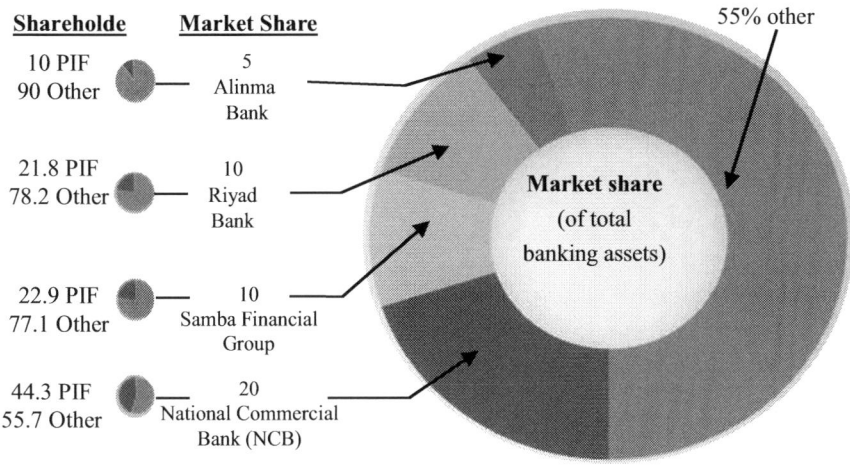

2.6 Implications of Rising Sovereign Domestic and Foreign Currency Debt   37

Shareholde	Market Share
10 PIF / 90 Other	5 Alinma Bank
21.8 PIF / 78.2 Other	10 Riyad Bank
22.9 PIF / 77.1 Other	10 Samba Financial Group
44.3 PIF / 55.7 Other	20 National Commercial Bank (NCB)

55% other

Market share (of total banking assets)

Source: Roll, 2019

Fig. 2.2 The PIF as a player in the Saudi banking sector—May 2019 (all figures in percentage). Source: Roll (2019)

Such a significant level of PIF banking asset ownership ensures that SAMA-PIF cooperation becomes even more critical, especially in light of the planned mega merger of NCB and SAMBA in October 2020 that will transfer all SAMBA's assets to NCB with SAMBA ceasing to exit as of 1st April 2021. The combined entity, to be named the Saudi National Bank, will become the largest bank in Saudi Arabia with more than SR 837 billion ($223 billion) in assets, and 25% of the retail and wholesale banking market. Some will argue that the planned merger will unlock a large synergy in the long run and sends a positive signal for a sector where the existing number of banks are presumably greater than the local economy, and as a means of enhancing efficiency and competitiveness of local banks as Saudi Arabia opens its doors to foreign banks. Mergers however can also be detrimental to competition, as customer choice will become more limited, as well as raising the specter of "too big to fail "to support such banks by the government in times of financial crisis.

2.6 Implications of Rising Sovereign Domestic and Foreign Currency Debt

As noted earlier, the need to tap into SAMA's stock of reserves can be optimized against a degree of fiscal consolidation and access to the international debt market, and an improvement in oil prices will also reduce the need to tap into Saudi reserves. For the time being, and in face of a global 2020 economic slowdown and COVID-19 disruptions, oil price recovery is somewhat of a lower priority to sustain reserves.

The continued implementation of the Vision 2030, has ensured that the forecasted Saudi budget deficit for 2021 is now estimated at SR 298 billion or 12% of GDP compared with SR 187 billion or 6.4% of GDP for 2020, with expectations that the fiscal deficit to progressively narrow to less than 1% by 2023. Public debt is expected to grow in line with government forecasts between 2021 and 22 and total SR 1029 trillion in 2023 or 31.8% of GDP (Jadwa Investment 2020).

Until recently, Saudi Arabia did not face significant funding gaps and the country did not need to develop any expertise in public debt management. This was until the steep fall in oil prices from 2015 causing fiscal deficits as the government had to borrow more than the revenues it received from oil. In order to have a more centralized process on the country's debt program, Saudi Arabia established in 2016 a Debt Management Office (DMO) in the Ministry of Finance to develop a comprehensive public debt management framework. With the assistance of the IMF, the DMO was established with responsibility for developing the legal, governance and risk management frameworks for debt management and also to promote debt management policies and practices that facilitate local debt market development, as the Kingdom has had a short history of deficit financing. From 1983 to 1988 the budget deficit, resulting from falling oil revenues, was financed out of state reserves but since mid-1988 government securities have been issued in the domestic market to fund fiscal deficits, first through the so-called 'Bankers Security Deposit Accounts'—BSDA's or Central Bank bills in mid-1980s, and then through Government Development Bonds issued since mid-1988. The BSDA's were replaced by SAMA Treasury bills in different maturities, of 1, 4, 13, 26 and 52-week bills (Jasser and Banafe 2003; Ramady 2010; Abalkhail 2002).

Government debt totaled around SR 820 billion ($218.7 bn) at the end of H1 2020, from both domestic and international borrowing as set out in Table 2.10 below.

Table 2.10 Saudi Government Debt rises significantly—domestic and foreign H1 2020

Item/period	(SR billion)		
(A) Deficit financing	Q1	Q2	Total
• Deficit	(34.107)	(109.236)	(143.344)
• Current Acct.	9.0	–	9.0
• Govt. reserves	–	48.668	48.668
• Domestic borrowing	11.194	29.924	41.118
• External borrowing	18.494	26.064	44.556
Total financing	38.688	104.064	143.344
(B) Public debt	**Domestic**	**External**	
• Beginning of period	(677.925)		
• Balance	372.764	305.161	
• Issuance/borrowing	96.941	45.000	
• Repayments	0	0	
End of period balance	469.705	350.161	
H1 2020	819.866		

Source: Ministry of Finance (2020)

2.6 Implications of Rising Sovereign Domestic and Foreign Currency Debt

The ratio of domestic to external public debt as of 1H 2020 is 57%, but it is the increased rate of external borrowing that is now more evident as a DMO strategy as noted from the larger amounts of external financing for both Q1 and Q2 2020 in Table 2.9. There are several reasons for this shift in direction, ranging from 'crowding out' the private sector as banks lend more to the government and reduce lending to the private sector, as well as the Saudi government still attracting significant international investor interest at competitive prices.

As noted from Table 2.10, the Q2 2020 fiscal deficit amounted to SR 109 billion but the H1 2020 deficit has now reached SR 143 billion and rising, with forecasts that by the end of the year 2020 this will have increased to around SR 363 billion or 13.5% of GDP (Jadwa Investment 2020). With SR 176 billion of the deficit is expected to be financed via debt, the remainder of the deficit, SR 186 billion might have to be financed through SAMA reserve drawdowns, as around SR 49 billion was used during H1 2020. According to *Tadawul*, there has also been a rise in listed local *sukuks* and bonds issued by corporates, paying higher interest rates than government bonds/*sukuks*, with 72 corporate bonds and *sukuks* listed by Q2 2020. The total local debt market size, both private and government, stood at SR 392.2 billion or $104 billion (Tadawul 2020).

It is not only the steady rise in public debt, whether domestic or foreign, that is a worrying long-term trend, with some forecasting this to reach around $304 billion by 2022 or nearly 37% of GDP (HSBC 2020), but also the burden of future interest payment on this accumulated debt, and repayments coming due as Table 2.10 indicated no repayments made during H1 2020. The DMO office has endeavored to spread its debt across the curve by opting for longer maturities in a bid to avoid a bunching effect and crowding for refunding, and now has bonds maturity in 20, 30 and even 40-years. The attractive international investment appetite for Saudi debt, albeit at increased yields, has also prompted both the PIF and Saudi Aramco to consider raising international debt in their own name in 2021.

While the level of national debt has been rising, national revenue has also decreased with government revenue totaling SR 134 billion in Q2 2020, down 49% year-on-year, with declines in both oil and non-oil revenues (Jadwa Investment 2020). Non-oil revenue, which is the hope for a more diversified Saudi economy, declined by 55% compared with the same period in Q2 2019, attributable to a combination of a deferral in various tax payments, municipality taxes, and the COVID-19 pandemic induced downturn in general economic activity. The Saudi government reacted by cutting back on expenses, which declined by 17% year-on-year to SR 243 billion but saw increased expenditures in healthcare. The Saudi government though made a bold decision to raise Value Added Tax (VAT) by 10% to 15% in July 2020—the biggest ever tax hike and out of step with the other GCC countries that remained at 5% VAT rates creating a dichotomy in inter-GCC fiscal and monetary policy alignment. As will be discussed later, the VAT rate was reduced to 5% in the real estate sector in October 2020 to stimulate that sector (Arab News 2020b). By mid-November 2020, the Saudi government seemed to leave the door open to review the VAT increase after COVID 19 pandemic ends so as to boost economic recovery after the VAT tax increase boosted inflation from 0.5% in June 2020 to 6.1% in July, but later statements by the Minister of Finance indicated that this might not happen for some time.

Reducing government expenditure, postponing non-critical infrastructure projects could assist in balancing the budget, but governments around the world have also taken measures in consolidating public sector revenues in a Treasury Consolidate accounts (TCA) or Treasury Single Accounts (TSA). In Saudi Arabia, government agencies had some discretion in maintaining operating accounts with Saudi commercial banks and disburse from them. Many of these accounts are current accounts and government deposits constitute a significant element of Saudi Commercial bank deposits, around SR 400.2 billion out of total customer deposits of SR 1865.9 billion or 21% (SAMA 2020b). Consolidating these in a Treasury Consolidated Account could provide the Ministry of Finance additional liquidity to disburse funds instead of raising more debt. However, doing so in a hasty manner would create unintended negative consequences to the affected Saudi banks in terms of liquidity pressure, lower profitability and reduced participation in Saudi Arabia's Vision 2030 project lending. To counter some of these effects, a close coordination with SAMA could help to mitigate a negative impact through the use of some of SAMA's monetary and macro prudential polices. Key policies that can be amended include:

- *Changes to SAMA current required reserve (RR) ratios* which stands at 7% for current accounts and 4% for time deposits. Most developed economies have either very low reserve requirements (EU countries at 1%, Japan 0.8%) while others (UK, Australia, Canada, Sweden) have gone to the other extreme with a voluntary reserve ratio or zero reserves.
- *Increasing Saudi banks' loans to deposit ratio* from 90% to 95% levels to allow for increased lending capacity,
- *Adjusting the current 20% statutory liquidity ratio* to 15%, freeing liquid assets to lending.

Of the above, changing the statuary reserve requirement can have a powerful money multiplier effect in increased money supply through the effects of the marginal propensity to consume multiplier (MPC), with a higher MPC leading to an increase in the money multiplier.

References

Abalkhail, M. (2002). *The role of fiscal policy in realizing the vision*. Riyadh: Centre for Economic and Management Studies, Future Vision of Saudi Arabia.

Abdeen, A and Dale, S. (1984). *The Saudi Finacial System in the context of Western and Islamic Finance*. New York, NY: John Wiley & Sons.

Ahmed, S. Z. (2012). Micro, small and medium sized enterprises development in the Kingdom of Saudi Arabia: Problems and Constraints. *World Journal of Entrepreneurship Management, Management and Sustainable Development, 8*(4), 217–232.

References

Al Rashidi, A., & Baakeel, O. (2012). The impact of operational risk management on the financial development and economic growth: A case study of Saudi SME companies. *European Journal of Business and Management, 4*(5).

Altokhais, S. (2017). Factors related to the financial assistance of SME's through the KAFALA programs in Saudi Arabia. *Journal of Contemporary Scientific Research, 2.*

Anderson, R. (2018). Saudi's *Shoura* Council approves Law granting the PIF greater independence. *Gulf Business.* Retrieved December 6, 2018 from www.gulfbusiness.com

Arab News. (2020a). *Crown prince salutes 'unprecedented' Saudi achievements.* Retrieved November 13, 2020, from www.arabnews.com

Arab News. (2020b). *Saudi Arabia brings in lower property tax to boost sector.* Retrieved October 2, from www.arabnews.com

Arab News. (2021). *Saudi Cabinet approves establishing Bank of SME's.* Arab News. Retrieved February 16, 2021 from www.arabnews.com

Argaam. (2016). *Central Bank changes name to Saudi Arabian Monetary Authority.* Retrieved December 4, 2016, from www.argaam.com

Argaam. (2020a). "*Credit Agricole Exit Banque Saudi Fransi, Sells Final Stake for SR 1.4 bn Sources*". 28 Sept. 2020. www.argaam.com

Argaam. (2020b). *Saudi Banks credit provisions rise 50% to SR 3.38 Bn in Q3 2020.* Retrieved November 15, 2020, from www.argaam.com

Argaam. (2021). *Changes to SAMA not to affect core functions: clear mechanism for surplus distribution: Al Jadaan.* Retrieved February10, 2021. www.argaam.com

Banafa, A., & Macleod, R. (2017). *The Saudi Arabian Monetary Agency 1952–2016: Central Bank of Oil.* London: Palgrave Macmillan.

Batlay, G. W., & Sendan E. (2002). *Financial sector reforms: international experience and issues for Saudi Arabia.* Riyadh: World Bank. Future Vision of Saudi Arabia.

Bloomberg. (2020). *PIF-Saudi transfers $40 billion to wealth fund.* New York: Bloomberg.

Dukheil, A. M. (1995). *The banking system and its performance in Saudi Arabia.* London: Saqi Books.

Essayyad, M., Ramady, M., & Al Hejji, M. (2003). Determinants of bank profitability of petroleum economy: The case of Saudi Arabia. *Petroleum Accounting and Financial Management Journal, 22*(3), 69–101.

Fayez, K. (2002). *Future role for banks and Saudi financial markets under the globalization of the economy.* Riyadh: Future Vision of Saudi Arabia.

Forbes. (2020). Saudi's 2020 investments so far. *Forbes*, from Mideast.com

Gamal El Din, Y., & Nereim, V. (2020). Saudi Arabia wont tap Debt Market again in 2020 "Minister says". *Bloomberg*, Retrieved November 20, 2020.

HSBC. (2020). *CEEMA economics.* HSBC Global Research. Q4 2020, from www.research.hsbc.com

Jadwa Investment. (2019). *SME's and vision 2020.* Jadwa Investment. Retrieved March 2019, from www.Jadwa.com

Jadwa Investment. (2020). *2021 Preliminary budget statement.* Jadwa Investment. Retrieved October 2020, from www.jadwa.com

Jasser, M. (2002). *Developing the financial Sector for better economic growth.* Riyadh: SAMA. Future Vision of Saudi Arabia.

Jasser, M. A., & Banafe, A. (2003). *Monetary policy investments and procedures in Saudi Arabia.* Riyadh: Saudi Arabian Monetary Agency (SAMA).

Kingdom of Saudi Arabia. (2017). *The public investment fund program 2018–2020.* from www.pif.gov.sa

Knight, M. (1998). Developing countries and the globalization of financial markets. *World Development, 26*(7), 1185–1200.

Martin, M, & Abu Omar, A. (2020). Saudi Arabia broadens Central Bank's mandate to promote growth. *Bloomberg*, Retrieved November 26, 2020.

Ministry of Finance (2020). *Budget Statement 2020.* Ministry of Finance, Riyadh. www.mof.gov.sa

Patrick, H. T. (1996). Financial development and economic growth in underdeveloped countries. *Economic Development and Capital Change, 14*(2), 174–177.

Radwan, R. (2021). *Crown Prince announces 5 year strategy for Kingdom's economy*. Retrieved January 24, 2021. Arab News, www.arabnews.com

Rafiki, A. (2019). Determinants of SME growth: An empirical study in Saudi Arabia. *International Journal of Organizational Analysis, 2019*. https://doi.org/10.1108/ijoa-02-2019-1665.

Ramady, M. A. (2010). *The Saudi Arabian economy: Policies, achievements and challenges*. New York: Springer International.

Reuters. (2019). *Saudi Arabia's NCB, Riyad Bank pull plug on merger plan*. Retrieved December 16, 2019, from www.reuters.com

Roll, S. (2019). *A sovereign wealth fund for the Prince: Economic reforms and power consolidation in Saudi Arabia*. German Institute for International and Security Affairs. SWP Research Paper No. 8, July, Berlin.

SAMA. (1960). *Annual Report 1960*. SAMA, Riyadh. Retrieved from www.sama.gov.sa

SAMA. (2004). *A case study on globalization and the role of institution building in the financial sector in Saudi Arabia*. Riyadh: SAMA.

SAMA. (2020a). *Various annual reports, 1960, 2009, and 2020 monthly statistical report*. Retrieved August, from www.sama.com

SAMA. (2020b). *King's approval for the Saudi Central Bank Law and change of name of the Saudi Arabian Monetary Authority*. Retrieved November 24, 2020, from www.sama.gov.sa

Saudi Gazette. (2020). *Central Bank allowed to buy properties to diversify its foreign investments*. Retrieved December 2, 2020, from www.saudigazette.com

Saudi Press Agency. (2016). *Custodian of the two holy mosques directs to allocate SR 100 billion from Kingdom's reserves to PIF account*. Riyadh: Saudi Press Agency.

Saudi Press Agency. (2020). *Shoura convened, formed specialized committees, endorsed Central Bank Law*. Retrieved November 16. 2020, from www.spa.gov.sa

Sheikh, S. (1999). Structure of Gulf banking and effects of globalization and financial liberalization. *The NCB Economist, 9*(2).

Suhaimi, J. (2002). *Consolidation, competition, foreign presence and systematic stability in the Saudi banking industry*. Riyadh: SAMA.

Tadawul. (2020). *Listing on the Saudi Stock market*. Riyadh: Tadawul.

Torchia, A., Kalin, S., & Rashad, M. (2018). Saudi's PIF invested in 50–60 firms via Softbank fund. *Reuters*, October 23.

Waked, B. (2016). *Access to finance by Saudi SME's- Constraints and the impact on their performance*. Australia: College of Business, Victoria University.

Wilson, R. (1983). *Banking and finance in the Arab Middle East*. London: Macmillan.

Chapter 3
The Saudi Capital Market: Coming of Age

He who has not the spirit of his age, has all the misery of it. Voltaire

Abstract The evolution and various stages of Saudi Capital Market reforms are examined, including the performance of the main *Tadawul* Stock Exchange and the *NOMU* parallel market. The initiatives to mobilize domestic and international investments and the financial leadership plans under the Vision 2030 are also explored, as well as the structure and composition of Saudi investment funds. The growth of new financial products such as the REIT's is examined as well as the role of the Saudi Real Estate Refinancing Company and relevant enforcement laws, given the importance of the Saudi mortgage sector.

Keywords Capital Market · *Tadawul* · *NOMU* · Foreign Investors · Vision 2030 Realization Plan · Mortgage · REIT's

3.1 Overview

Capital market reforms, particularly those aimed at encouraging international investor participation in the Saudi capital market have been a linchpin in unlocking the Kingdom's economic and investment potential. Today's Saudi capital market regulators and its operating structure is a far cry from the infancy days of the

1970s (Dukheil 1995; Abdeen and Shook 1984). Far ranging reforms undertaken by the Tadawul (Exchange) in conjunction with the Capital Market Authority (CMA), especially over the past 2 years have yielded significant results in terms of improved market function and efficiency, expanded access to international investors, enhanced corporate governance and increased transparency. All these have helped to align the Saudi capital market with international standards, making it more attractive to international investors, both directly and through passive investments once the *Tadawul* was included in key international indexes like the FTSE Russell, MSCI and S&P Dow Jones EM indexes. Saudi Arabia now constitutes 3.1% of the FTSE Emerging Index and 0.35% in the FTSE All-World Index (FTSE Russell 2020).

3.2 The Tadawul Stock Exchange: From a Humble Beginning to a Global Player

In 1954, the foundation was laid for an informal Saudi share trading market, and by the 1970s it continued as such with only 14 listed companies. By 1980, it acquired some semblance of a formal market as the 'Saudi Company for Share Registration' was officially established in 1984 after being regulated by a special ministerial committee. In 2003, SAMA established the Capital Market Authority as a regulator and facilitator body with the launch of the Electronic Securities Information System (ESIS). By 2007, SAMA relinquished this oversight and *Tadawul* was formed as a joint stock company and the sole entity authorized to act as a securities exchange, with further milestones in 2015 with the opening of the Saudi Capital Market to Qualified Foreign Investors (QFI's) and establishing the Securities Depository Center Company (EDAA) in 2016 and the Securities Clearing Center Company (MUQASSA) in 2018. In a further development , the Saudi Stock Exchange has announced that the *Tadawul* will launch its initial public offering—IPO—after 2021, but that it depended on the company's preparations and according to Tadawul's CEO Al Hussan, the planned IPO could take place within two years (Argaam 2020b, 2021). Today, the Public Investment Fund owns 100% of *Tadawul* as illustrated in Fig. 3.1 below.

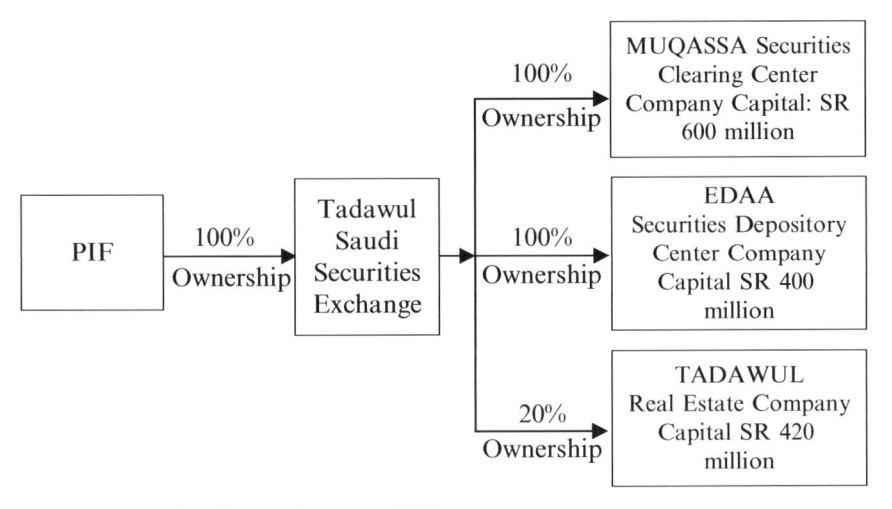

3.2 The Tadawul Stock Exchange: From a Humble Beginning to a Global Player

```
                                         ┌──────────────────────┐
                                         │ MUQASSA Securities   │
                                  100%   │ Clearing Center      │
                                ────────▶│ Company Capital: SR  │
                               Ownership │ 600 million          │
                                         └──────────────────────┘
┌─────┐           ┌──────────┐           ┌──────────────────────┐
│     │   100%    │ Tadawul  │           │ EDAA                 │
│ PIF │ ────────▶ │ Saudi    │   100%    │ Securities Depository│
│     │ Ownership │Securities│─────────▶ │ Center Company       │
│     │           │ Exchange │ Ownership │ Capital SR 400       │
└─────┘           └──────────┘           │ million              │
                                         └──────────────────────┘
                                         ┌──────────────────────┐
                                         │ TADAWUL              │
                                  20%    │ Real Estate Company  │
                                ────────▶│ Capital SR 420       │
                               Ownership │ million              │
                                         └──────────────────────┘
```

Source: Tadawul Annual Report 2019

Fig. 3.1 *Tadawul*'s ownership structure and operating entities 2020. Source: Tadawul Annual Report (2019)

By 10 October 2020, Saudi Market Capitalization stood at SR 8.23 trillion ($2.39 billion), ranked 58th out of 144 global stock markets, first in the Arab stock markets, and second largest after China when compared to top Emerging Markets, coming a long way in comparison with its capitalization of SR 254 billion in 2000, and SR 1.946 trillion in 2007. Compared with the 14 listed companies in the 1970s, today there are 199 listed companies with 41 companies listed during 2015–2019 alone, including the largest IPO in the world—*Saudi Aramco* in December 2019 at slightly above the desired $2 trillion level, although slipping back to between $1.8 and 1.9 trillion in 2020, affected by lower global oil prices, although Aramco was still committed to its promised dividend payout of $75 billion for 2020 (Sayigh and Gamal 2020). In a development that could further boost *Tadawul*, in 2021, Crown Prince Mohammed bin Salman announced during the annual Future Investment Initiative (FII) that Saudi Aramco could launch a second offering of shares to yield a cash flow to the PIF to be reinvested domestically and internationally but no indication on the size of the potential new offering or whether it will be listed on the Saudi Stock Exchange or include international listing (Kane 2021).

Tadawul's strategic plan is quite ambitious—to create an exchange with world-class investor solutions. The establishment of the Securities Clearing Center Company (Muqassa) role as an independent clearing house enables the achievement of a strategy by strengthening the market's post-trade infrastructure, provides centralized counterparty risk management and enables the introduction of new products and services. These included the introduction of exchange derivative trading in January 2020, listing of government *'Sukuk'* issuance in Aril 2018 and Exchange Traded Funds (ETF's) and Real Estate Investment Traded funds (REIT's) in 2020.

Within a space of 5 years—2015 to 2020—*Tadawul* has racked up a wide range of achievements, illustrated in Table 3.1 below:

Table 3.1 *Tadawul*'s major achievements 2015–2020

Date	Achievement
June 2015	• Launch of the Independent Custody Framework • Opening up the direct ownership of assets through the QF1 framework
Sep 2015	*Tadawul* Upgraded Trading Platform (X~Stream iNet)
Nov 2016	REITs listed the 1st Real Estate Investment fund
Jan 2017	Spin off the Security and Depository Centre (Edaa)
Jan 2017	Global Industry Classification Standard—GICS new classification system adopted by *Tadawul*
Feb 2017	Parallel Market (NOMU) Launch of the parallel market
April 2017	• Shift from T+0 settlement cycle to T+2 settlement cycle • Securities lending and short selling framework • Transfer of Regulatory Responsibilities of Exchange from Regulator
Apr 2018	Listing of Government Sukuk Issuances
Mar–Jul 2018	Classified as an emerging market in three major indices: MSCI. FTSE Russel, and S&P Global
Aug 2018	The approval of First Trading and Membership Rules
Jan 2019	*Tadawul* & MSCI launch MSCI *Tadawul* (MT30) Joint Index
Mar 2019	Establish Securities Clearing Center *Muqassa*
Aug/Sep 2019	Completion of the inclusion In MSCI & S&P
Nov 2019	Capital Market Law approved by council of ministers (CCP Recognition)
Dec 2019	ARAMCO Listing: *Tadawul* among the Top Ten Exchange in Market Cap
Jan 2020	Approval of: • Exchange Derivatives Trading & Membership Rules and Procedures • Securities Clearing Center Rules, and Cleaning Procedures
Jan 2020	*Muqassa* Obtains the First License in Saudi Arabia to Clear Securities as a Qualified Center Counterparty (QCCP)
Jun 2020	Completion of the Inclusion in FTSE Russell
Aug. 2020	Launch of Derivative Market with SF 30 index futures contract Commencement of securities Clearing Center Company's (*Muqasaa*) operations

Source: CMA (2020)

The launching of the *Tadawul* derivative market with SF 30 Index Futures contracts and approval of exchange derivative trading in January, 2020 was preceded by SAMA's rules on trade repository reporting and risk mitigation requirements for Over the Counter (OTC) derivatives contracts in November 2019, to introduce reforms in response to G20 commitment to regulate the OTC derivatives markets in the aftermath of the global financial crisis. The G20 Summit in Pittsburgh, USA in September 2009 resolved to take measures to reduce risk in the financial system, and, in particular, to minimize the risk of contagion from OTC derivative markets.

As of 1 January 2020, when the *Tadawul* approved Exchange Derivatives trading, all SAMA regulated banks, including SAMA—regulated branches of foreign banks are required to report details of their outstanding OTC interest rate derivatives or OTC foreign exchange that are cleared or uncleared to a SAMA authorized trade repository on a daily basis. Derivatives transactions where the counterparty is the Saudi Arabian government, SAMA, the *Tadawul*, the Depository Center, a supranational authority, a multilateral development bank or an insurance company do not need to be reported by a Saudi bank. The outcome of all initiatives is that it highlights the close working relationship between SAMA and the Saudi CMA, where regulatory changes are coordinated.

3.3 Mobilizing Local and Foreign Investment: Developing an Advanced Capital Market

The Capital Market Authority has been in the forefront to ensure that both domestic and foreign investors can have confidence in participating in the local stock market and has taken several key initiatives as part of its objectives to realize part of the financial programs of Vision 2030.

A number of developments have supported the advancement of the Saudi capital market since the launch of the Financial Sector Development Program (FSDP) with one major change being the removal of a cap on ownership for foreign strategic investors in listed companies, which was previously limited to 49%, but now can hold majority of listed shares, but that foreign strategic investors are required to hold onto shares for at least 2 years following the date of ownership to avoid speculative volatility. One of the metrics under the FSDP 2020 commitment states that foreign qualified investor ownership, as a percentage of the Saudi equity market capitalization should be a minimum of 10% at the end of 2019, rising to a minimum of 15% in 2020. Given the *Tadawul*'s inclusion in the MSCI Emerging market and FTSE Emerging market indexes in 2020 the Saudi Capital Market Authority feels confident that these targets will be surpassed, but as noted in Table 3.2 below, the CMA has some ambitious strategic targets to meet.

Table 3.2 Key CMA strategic leadership plans under vision 2030 Financial Sector Development Program (FSDP)

Performance indicator	Baseline year	Baseline value	Unit	Actual 2018	Target 2019	Target 2020	Target 2021
Market capitalization (shares & debt instruments) as a percentage of GDP (%)	2016	78%	%	83%	86.75%=<	88%=<	88.70%=<
Assets under Management (AUM) as a percent out of GDP (%)	2016	12%	%	17%	18%=<	22%=<	24%=<
Market concentration of top 10 companies by market cap	2016	57%	%	62%	56%	55%	55%
Institutional investors' share of value traded (%)	2016	18%	%	27.4%	19%=<	20%=<	20%=<
Foreign Investor Ownership of the equity market cap (%)	2016	4%	%	4.70%	10%=<	15%=<	15%=<
Number of micro & small companies listed as a percent out of total number of listed companies (%)	2016	30%	%	42%	39%=<	40%=<	40%=<
Share of investment accounts opened through eKYC (%)	–	–	%	–	5%	10%	12%
Volatility of the Saudi Stock market index (average volatility of 90 days)	2016	21.76	Rate	13.9	25=<	25=<	25=<
Minimum free float of equity market cap in % of total outstanding shares (%)	2016	42%	%	42.8%	45%=<	45%=<	45%=<
Total amounts raised from offering securities (shares, debt, REITs, PE funds, VC funds, financing funds)	2016	430	SR billion (Accum)	197	375	506	630
Number of annually listed companies in Saudi shares market	2016	4	Nb	12	22	23	25
Growth rate of market institutions sector' revenues	2016	−16%	% Accum.	9.2%	30%	50%	60%
The avg. of violation resolution time from the time of discovery and until its disposal within the CMA	2016	10	Months	7.2	5	3.5	3
The average period of time for litigation in securities disputes	2016	28	Months	12.9	12	9	7

Source: Jadwa Investment (2019)

3.3 Mobilizing Local and Foreign Investment: Developing an Advanced Capital Market

Assessing the CMA's performance indicators, these can be broadly grouped in two sectorial targets: those that can be relatively managed by the CMA, and those that are affected by external factors outside the control of the CMA but can be influenced by government actions. Those that the CMA can relatively manage include:

- *Share of investment accounts opened through eKYC*
- *Number of annually listed companies in Saudi shares market (albeit that this will be affected by the general economic outlook and investor confidence),*
- *The average period of time for litigation in securities disputes,*
- *The average of violation resolution time from the time of discovery and until its disposal within the CMA,*
- *Number of micro and small companies listed as a percent out of total number of listed companies.*

External factors such as oil price volatility, COVID 19 outbreak economic impact, and geo-political risks in the Gulf region will affect these CMA Vision 2030 FSDP program indicators:

- Market capitalization as percentage of GDP,
- Assets under management
- Foreign investor ownership of the equity market
- Volatility of the Saudi stock market index,
- Total amounts raised from offering securities.

One other indicator, market concentration of top 10 companies by market capitalization, such as the planned NCB and SAMBA mega bank merger announced in October 2020, is outside the CMA's auspices and under another regulator (SAMA), but the CMA has the necessary regulatory tools to investigate undue market concentration and anti-competitive practices. Despite not having total control over Vision 2030 performance indicators, the CMA's main initiatives in facilitating financing, encouraging investment and enhancing confidence is set out in Table 3.3 below.

Table 3.3 CMA and vision 2030 realization

2030 Initiatives	Purpose	Outcome
(A) Facilitating Financing	(1) Deeping the capital market and enhancing its role in capital formation (2) Developing the *Sukuk* and debt market instruments	• Amendment of rules for Qualified Foreign Financial Institutions Investment in the listed securities • Amendment of the merger and acquisitions regulation • Listing of debt instruments issued by Govt. of Saudi Arabia
(B) Encouraging investment	(1) Enhancing market attractiveness to foreign investors	• Inclusion of *Tadawul* in MSCI, FTSE Russell and S&P Dow Jones emerging market indexes
(C) Enhancing confidence	(1) Enhancing the regulatory environment of the capital market (2) Increasing transparency and disclosure in the capital market	• Launch of the investor protection application • Separating the duties between CMA and *Tadawul* • Adoption of the rules for registering Auditors of Entities Subject to the Authority Supervision

Source: CMA (2020)

The result of these reforms and regulatory oversight has attracted private sector investors as well as a wide range of funds set up to meet all type of client liquidity and risk profiles. As of H2 2020 there were a total of 301 traded funds, of which 118 were 'public funds' and 183 'private funds'. The latter are deemed riskier whose units are offered to qualified investors through private placements in accordance to the Investment Funds Regulations issued by the CMA. Public funds have more regulatory oversight and also on who can participate. Table 3.4 summarizes the availability of both type of funds.

Table 3.4 Public and private Saudi Investment Funds by type and ownership 2020

Fund type	Public		Private	
	Local	Foreign	Local	Foreign
Equity	36	–	22	2
Multi asset	2	–	16	–
Money market	26	–	19	2
Real estate	8	–	37	6
Private equity	–	–	30	9
Hedge	–	–	4	2
Debt/bond	9	–	8	1
Commodity	1	–	4	–
Feeder fund	1	–	5	–
Margin lending	–	–	3	–
Indirect financing	–	–	1	–
Fixed income	–	–	6	–
Venture capital	–	–	5	–
Endowment	3	–	1	–
Index	1	–	–	–
Fund of funds	9	–	–	–
REIT	15	–	–	–
ETF	4	–	–	–
Index	1	–	–	–
Balanced	2	–	–	–
Total	118	–	161	22

Source: Tadawul (2020)

Analysis of the composition of private and public funds indicates the predominance of 'traditional' investments in equity, money market and in the specialized REIT real estate funds. The funds of choice in the private funds were focused in private equity, real estate and equity, with money market and multi-asset also popular. Foreign run private funds focused on private equity and real estate.

The popularity of investment funds is demonstrated in the rapid increase in both the number of subscribers and the total assets held by these funds over the past 5 years 2015–2020 as illustrated in Table 3.5 below, which also sets out closed and open-ended funds.

Table 3.5 Saudi investment funds by number, subscribers, domestic and foreign assets, total value and open/closed categories (2015–2020)

Period	No. of operating funds	No. of subscribers	Domestic assets (SR Bn)	Foreign assets (SR Bn)	Total assets of funds (SR Bn)	Open ended funds		Closed ended funds	
						Number	Assets (SR Bn)	Number	Assets (SR Bn)
2015	270	236,977	75.9	26.9	102.8	261	100.5	9	2.3
2016	275	224,411	70.6	17.2	87.7	263	84.9	1212	2.8
2017	273	238,445	91.1	19.1	110.2	255	98.3	18	11.9
2018	249	332,567	93.6	18.2	111.9	223	87.4	26	24.5
2019	253	329,739	133.4	26.5	159.9	228	133.2	25	26.7
Q3 2020	255	358,576	148.8	47.3	196.0	230	167.9	25	28.1

Source: CMA (2020), SAMA (2020)

According to the CMA, which from 2006 has provided the main source of data to SAMA, total investment funds held in domestic assets as of Q3 2020 was SR 148.8 billion and SR 47.3 billion in foreign assets, totaling SR 196 billion, significantly up over the SR 102.8 billion in 2015. Table 3.5 indicates that the number of subscribers have increased by around 20,000 over the 5-year period, with a drop in 2016 of around 10,000 following a fall in the Saudi market index in late 2015, in line with other global and regional stock market retreats, and concerns about low oil prices from $68 a barrel in May 2016 to $45 a barrel in August 2016.

Of interest is that by Q3 2020, some SR 83.9 billion was invested in short-term money market instruments, or nearly 45% of total assets, followed by SR 38.9 billion invested in foreign money market instruments or around 18%. The third largest investment category component was unsurprisingly in domestic real estate investments of over SR 24.6 billion or 12.5%, with domestic shares at SR 19.0 billion or 9.6% (SAMA, Statistical Report, Sept. 2020). Other foreign assets comprising foreign shares, foreign bonds, and other foreign assets totaled SR 8.3 billion or 4.2%. With nearly 78% of total assets in domestic instruments, the Saudi investment funds subscribers seem to have clearly indicated their preferences for Saudi based investments.

3.4 The NOMU Parallel Market Adds Depth and Opportunity

In the first quarter of 2020, *Tadawul* also unveiled structural changes to the successful launch of the *NOMU*—(an Arabic word for growth)—parallel market, which is aimed at supporting the growth, development and sustainability of the SME focused market segment. The aim is clear-to increase the number of listed companies on

NOMU, enhance market liquidity and provide a viable platform for the SME's to transit to the main market when they grow in size, and meet key SME Vision 2030 objectives. According to the CMA, the main objectives in establishing the NOMU Parallel Market are as follows:

- Additional source of funding for issuers to access capital, and
- Increased diversification and deepening of the Saudi Capital market.

The criteria for listing and offering in *NOMU* are quite attractive to aspiring SME owners, and the key elements are:

1. *The issuer must be a joint stock company, in which majority of its capital is owned by citizens of a GCC member state,*
2. *Must have a minimum capitalization of SR 10 million (main market SR 300 million),*
3. *The issuer must float at least 20% of the issued shares at time of listing, or SR 30 million whichever is less,*
4. *Must have a minimum of 2 year of operational and financial performance,*
5. *Appointing a financial advisor is mandatory, legal advisor optional,*
6. *Annual audited financial statements,*
7. *Disclosure of significant/essential information,*
8. *At least 50 public shareholders are required at time of listing (main market 200),*
9. *No profitability track record required.*

Unlike the *Tadawul* Saudi Stock Exchange's main market, the *NOMU* Parallel market has less restrictive listing rules, thus giving a broader cross-section of Saudi companies the opportunity to have their shares publicly trade. In a further liberalization move , the CMA approved in December 2020 , the deregulation of the market institutions commission of buying and selling listed equities on the *NOMU* parallel market for both buyers and sellers (Argaam 2020a). *NOMU* has now provided an opportunity for ambitious SME's to address expansion plans and capital raising needs as well as enhancing their market profile and increase brand equity. Investment activities through the NOMU Parallel Market are restricted to "Qualified Investors" but investors may invest through qualifying investment funds offered by licensed investment companies. The results have been encouraging, with the *NOMU* index rising from 3200 in 2017 when it was launched, to stand at around 15,000 in October 2020. Capitalization has increased from $600 million in 2017 by $793 million by 2020 (*Tadawul* Annual Report 2019). The CMA has also introduced wholesale changes to *NOMU* in 2019, including allowing companies to directly list on NOMU's Technical Listing, allowing for companies to move from *NOMU* to the Main Market and moving towards a semi-annual disclosure regime. Other changes include reducing normal trade thresholds and index capping (Tadawul 2020).

3.5 Growth of New Financial Products and Market Players-REIT's

The Saudi financial market has now seen the entry of different players in some priority economic sectors, especially real estate, finance leasing, and FinTech Companies. SAMA has retained its regulatory responsibility in issuing licenses to participants in these sectors.

One of the more recent financial products that has rapidly expanded, has been the introduction of Real Estate Investment Traded Funds (REIT's), which have also been permitted in other emerging markets. For Saudi Arabia, besides their impact on broadening the capital market, REIT's can also help to realize the broader goals of the National Transformation Program of the Vision 2030 and increase the real estate sector's contribution to GDP (Jadwa Investment 2016). REIT's can also facilitate the participation of the private sector in developing vacant land plots and raising the supply of real estate, The Saudi REIT's are closed-ended investment companies which own income-producing real estate. As noted earlier from Table 3.4, there are presently 15 public REIT's as well as another 8 real estate funds, while there were 37 private real estate funds in Saudi Arabia, highlighting the attractiveness of the real estate sector for Saudi investors. The promotion of Riyadh, the Saudi capital into the ranks of the top 10 largest city economies in the world by 2030, as announced during the 2021 FII Conference will only accelerate the attractiveness of current and new Saudi REIT's, with the number of forecasted residents of Riyadh increasing from 7.5 million to 15-20 million by 2030 (Amlot 2021). The Saudi REIT's are regulated by SAMA and have the following requirements:

- *Minimum of SR 500 million offered,*
- *1 year lock up period*
- *30% of the REIT owned by the public but excludes any unit holders owning 5% or more REIT units, at least 200 public unit holders,*
- *A minimum of 75% of total assets value should be invested in income producing real estate,*
- *A maximum of 25% of total fund's asset value can be invested in real estate development, renovating and redevelopment of properties,*
- *A maximum of 25% of a REIT's total value can be invested outside the Kingdom,*
- *At least 90% of the funds net income must be distributed annually,*
- *Leverage 50 % of NAV at a maximum,*
- *Foreign QFI's are able to participate in Saudi REIT's.*

The Saudi government has made it clear in its Vision 2030 objectives that one of its priorities is increasing the supply of residential real estate home ownership to 70% by 2030, as in the past few years, Saudi home ownership was on a downward trend from 62% in 2007 to around 43% in 2016 due to a rapidly rising population, a lack of supply of sufficient residential units and the absence of financial products to facilitate home ownership. A tax on underdeveloped land imposed in 2017 has increased available land supply.

The results have been significant, with total number of new mortgage contracts rising sharply as illustrated in Fig. 3.2 below.

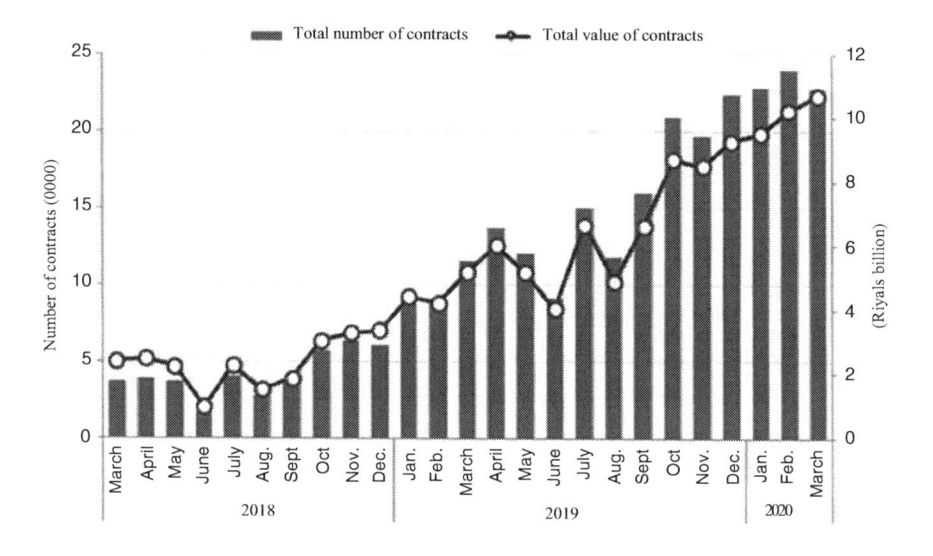

Source: Saudi Arabian Monetary Authority, Annual Reports.

Fig. 3.2 New residential mortgages in Saudi Arabia (riyal billion) 2018–2020. (For individuals, provided by banks). Source: Saudi Arabian Monetary Authority, Annual Reports (2020)

According to SAMA, out of the 40,885 mortgage contracts in 2018, there were 21,995 for housing, and the popularity of these mortgage contracts increased to 130,743 contracts by Q2 2020 accounting for 48,428 housing mortgages (SAMA, Monthly Statistical Report, Aug. 2020). In order to accelerate lending to the mortgage sector, this was given a boost following SAMA's decision in January 2018 to raise the loan-to-value limit for real estate loans as noted earlier in the Chapter.

However, the COVID-19 pandemic and fall in oil prices in 1H 2020 has weighed on Saudi economic growth. The Saudi government's decision to raise VAT to 15% to boost non-oil revenues in 2020 was reversed in October 2020 when the Kingdom scrapped VAT on property deals and introduced a lower 5% real estate transaction tax, while granting licensed real estate developers the right to recover the VAT incurred on their goods and services which were subject to VAT. The government also announced that the state will bear the cost of the Real Estate Transaction Tax for first time homeowners up to SR 1 million ($267,000) for Saudi nationals (Arab News 2020).

Of long-term financing importance, Saudi Arabia has established the Saudi Real Estate Refinance Company (SRC) often compared with the USA's Fannie Mai, and is publicly owned mortgage Refinance Company through the PIF. Established in 2017 with an initial authorized equity of SR 5 billion, the SRC is currently capitalized at SR 1.5 billion and has deployed around SR 2.8 billion in mortgage refinancing as of H1 2020, 70% of which is portfolio purchases by the SRC. This is done by the SRC acquiring mortgage portfolios from Saudi banks to diversify their funding sources and more loans off their balance sheet, with the SRC assuming the durational and interest risk of long term fixed loans in the portfolios it acquires, with access to a broader set of hedging tools than domestic banks. Salary assignments for mortgage lending has been the determining factor for bank homeownership lending, but with banks exposed to salary risk rather than asset risk, this type of lending has favored Saudi public sector employees, than private sector employees, as the risk of job losses in the public sector is limited.

The absence of refinancing firms in the Saudi mortgage market had until recently limited the ability of banks to expand their loan books in any one sector, but with the establishment of the SRC, bank loan portfolios can be packaged into mortgage-backed securities and sold to investors, creating a secondary capital market investment outlet. As of H1 2020, the SRC was planning to buy more than SR 23 billion of mortgage portfolios from banks, compared with SR 2 billion in 2019. In light of the COVID 19 and economic slowdown, the SRC also reduced rates by 15 basis points for its long term fixed rate mortgages in April 2020, but of more significance, also announced a 'forbearance program' in May 2020 for private sector employees, especially in healthcare and self-employed citizens, allowing them the option to defer mortgage payments for at least three months without any additional costs.

3.6 Strengthening the Mortgage Financial Legal Framework

In order to build confidence to both domestic and international investors in the real estate finance market, SAMA has introduced a raft of laws to highlight the government's commitment towards enhancing homeownership and improving mortgage penetration rates in the Kingdom. The key objective is that for a well-functioning mortgage system to operate laws and regulations to provide lenders and borrowers with a reasonable degree of comfort and confidence in the system have to be in place. The following summarizes the real estate mortgage and financial laws enacted by SAMA since 2014:

- *The 'Enforcement Law'*: provides for judges to hear enforcement disputes and insolvency actions, allowing for possible foreclosure compliant with *Shariah* principles,
- *The Real Estate Finance Law*: provides the regulatory architecture for the authorization and licensing of banks and finance companies to enter the real estate market, with banks allowed to own real estate for purposes of real estate finance,
- *The Registered Real Estate Mortgage Law*: Allows for registration of real estate mortgages with the pledged asset fully described in the mortgage contract to avoid uncertainty or fraud.
- *The Finance Lease Law*: prescribes the rules surrounding finance leasing and specifically outlines the responsibilities of the lessor and lessee in a *Shariah* compliant manner, and the lessor is permitted to request payment of future rentals if the lessee is in payment default,
- *The Finance Companies Control Law*: provides a regulatory and supervisory framework for *Shariah* compliant finance companies to provide real estate financing including other SAMA approved forms of financing.

From the above, it becomes noticeable of the importance of *Shariah* compliance, and while the new 'Enforcement Law' grants judges the power to hand ownership of a property to the mortgage provider should a borrower default, there is little precedent in Saudi Arabia for the *Shariah* courts to seize properties, particularly if they are primary family home. While the above might be a barrier to real estate financing, the government has widened the ability of citizens to have access to finance with SAMA leading the way by raising the loan to value (LTV) ratio for financing companies to 85% compared to 70% introduced in 2014. This was followed in 2017 permitting 85% LTV cap for citizens seeking first home ownership through banks, and was further raised to 90% in 2018.

In a further significant move, in 2015 it was announced that the Real Estate Development Fund (REDF) would be turned into a bank offering mortgages for existing homes and for the development of new homes with REDF now providing a range of mortgage subsidies through banks including a guarantee worth 5% of the property value as down payment up to a maximum limit of SR 500,000. Additionally, in 2016 SAMA announced the development of subsidized mortgage products to finance housing for eligible citizens in coordination with the Ministry of Housing and the Ministry of Finance, with the borrower responsible for 15% for a down payment and lenders financing 70% and the remaining 15% guaranteed by the Ministry of Finance. To further boost Saudi nationals home ownership an 'affordable' housing program was launched in 2017 under the so-called, *'SAKANI*, Affordable Housing Program' by the Ministry of Housing, with mortgage loans, land plots and residential units allotted to Saudi beneficiaries. Other REDF bank initiatives under the Vision 2030 program includes:

- Housing support for active military personnel,
- Lease-to-own for beneficiaries not entitled to housing support in form of subsidized lease installments,
- Down payment zero-interest subsidy program for beneficiaries over 45 years and on a salary less than SR 14,000 ($3733) p.a., with a maximum loan of SR 140,000 repayable at end of the funding period,
- Cooperative program with the Ministry of Finance to facilitate housing loans for government employees by issuing official guarantees for bank loans granted to applicants in the public sector.

All the above initiatives and perceived market attractiveness due to the young age profile of the Saudi population, has ensured that other private sector real estate financing players as well as non—real estate finance companies, extend significant credit to the sector. This reached SR 41 billion in assets by Q3 2020, or nearly 93% of total real estate assets compared with SR 2.8 billion of assets held by the Saudi Refinance Company, a mere 7%. It is envisaged that more real estate financing companies will enter the market, given relatively high returns with average return on equity of around 8%.

References

Abdeen, A., & Shook, D. (1984). *The Saudi financial system in the context of Western and Islamic finance*. New York: John Wiley & Sons.

Amlot, M. (2021) *Saudi Crown Prince reveals plans for Riyadh to be top 10 largest city economy in world*. Retrieved January 28, 2021. Al Arabiya. www.alarabiya.net

Arab News. (2020). *Saudi Arabia brings in lower property tax to boost sector*. Retrieved October 2, from www.arabnews.com

Argaam. (2020a). *CMA deregulates market institutions trading commission on NOMU*. Retrieved December 1, 2020, from www.argaam.com

Argaam. (2020b). *Tadawul to go public after 2020, says Al Hussan*. Retrieved December 11, 2020, from www.argaam.com

Argaam. (2021). *Tadawul to unveil IPO plans in 2021 says CEO Al Hussan*. Retrieved January 28, 2021. www.argaam.com

CMA. (2020). *Annual reports*. Riyadh: Various Years, Capital Market Authority, from www.cma.gov.sa

Dukheil, A. M. (1995). *The banking system and its performance in Saudi Arabia*. London: Saqi Books.

FTSE Russell. (2020). FTSE Russell completes inclusion of Saudi Arabian stock to its global equity index series. *Press Release*, 22 June.

Jadwa Investment. (2016). *Real Estate Investment Traded Funds (REIT's)*. Jadwa Investment. Retrieved December, from www.jadwa.com

Jadwa Investment. (2019). *SME's and Vision 2020*. Jadwa Investment. Retrieved March 2019, from www.Jadwa.com

Kane, F. (2021). *Aramco could sell more shares to benefit PIF, Saudi Crown Prince tells FII*. Retrieved January 28, 2021. Arab News. www.arabnews.com

Saudi Arabian Monetary Agency (SAMA). (2020). *Various annual reports, 1960, 2009, and 2020 monthly statistical report*. Retrieved August, from www.sama.com

Sayigh, H., & Gamal, R. (2020). Saudi Aramco profits falls 25% but dividend in line with planned payout for year. *Reuters*, Retrieved May 12, 2020.

Tadawul. (2019). *Annual report*. Riyadh: Tadawul, from www.tadawul.com.sa

Tadawul. (2020). *Listing on the Saudi stock market*. Riyadh: Tadawul, from www.tadawul.com.sa

Chapter 4
Unfinished Business, Challenges Ahead and Conclusion

Your old men shall dream dreams, your young men shall see visions.
Joel 2:28 KJV

Abstract Various SAMA and government measures to mitigate COVID-19 effects are examined, as well as FDI inflows over time and its importance to implement Saudi Arabia Vision 2030 program. The Vision 2030 Financial Plan and its adjustment in the COVID era is assessed, as well as key pillars are examined. The long planned GCC Monetary Union is revisited and whether it would take place in face of national autonomy concerns and differing GCC pegged currency policies. The G20 Saudi Presidency is examined as well as the workings of the various G20 specialist tracks and Saudi stakeholder participation and initiatives in circular carbon economy implementation. Future challenges facing Saudi Arabia are examined exam including rising debt concerns and prospects for economic diversification.

Keywords COVID-19 · FDI · Vision 2030 Financial Plan · GCC Monetary Union · G20 · Aramco · *Kafalah* · Circular Carbon Economy · Oil Price · OPEC

4.1 Overview

The latest Saudi labor market data indicates a jump in unemployment to 15.4% in Q2 2020, up from 11.8% in Q1, 2020 with female unemployment rising faster than male. The COVID-19 economic damage is beginning to make itself felt, with the number of expats declining by 19,000 in Q2 2020 with most sectors seeing a decline in the number of Saudis and expat workers in Q2 2020 (Jadwa Investment 2020a).

The various measures the government is taking to counter COVID-19 will take time to take effect, but until then, slower economic activity will put further pressure on state reserves and/or induce additional national debt borrowing.

To meet these challenges, as well as FinTech competition from foreign banks, some Saudi banks could contemplate mergers, especially amongst the larger financial institutions, with repercussions for the smaller Saudi banks, who will then need to reinvent themselves to re-contemplate what their business model should be—whether boutique banks that specialize in certain services like *Shariah* compliant or real estate. This has already happened with Gulf International Bank, owned nearly 98% by the PIF, which launched its *"Meem"* in 2015, the first *Shariah* compliant digital banking service in the region. As noted earlier, NCB and SAMBA Financial Group signed a definitive legally binding agreement in October 2020 which will transform the Saudi banking landscape and cause major industry concentration. The combined assets of the merged entities which will be known as, the Saudi National Bank, would be SR 762 billion ($203 billion) out of a total sector 2019 asset base of SR 2445 billion ($652 billion) or 31% of total banking assets. The PIF's ownership in the merged banks would become 37.2%, creating a truly significant Saudi and Gulf "super bank" (Argaam 2020b). SAMA's attitude towards such merger moves was summarized by former SAMA Governor Ahmad Al Kholifey in June 2020 when he was quoted as saying that SAMA does not mind mergers between Saudi banks if it serves the sector and the economy.

On a positive note, Moody's has in October 2020 assigned an A1/Aaa rating to the most recent *Sukuk* instrument issued under the domestic issuance program, which according to the Ministry of Finance, reflects the strength of the Kingdom's economy and ability to confront global economic challenges in the current extraordinary circumstances endured by the world. According to the National Debt Management Office, the move by Moody's showed the depth of the local debt market by providing a risk-free yield curve.

As part of its responsibilities, SAMA introduced a wide support program with a total value of SR 50 billion to support the private sector to spur economic growth as part of its role in activating monetary policy tools to enhance financial stability in the Saudi economy, and especially enabling the financial sector to support the private sector. Main SAMA measures in response to the COVID-19 outbreak include:

- *Deferred Payment Program* to support the financing of SME's by offering SR 30 billion to banks and finance companies to delay loan payments due from SME's for a period of 6 months,
- *Funding for lending program* totaling SR 13.2 billion to support business continuity during the pandemic,
- *Loan Guarantee Program (Kafalah)* of SR 6 billion to support financing of SME's to exempt SME's from paying the *Kafalah* fees,
- *POS and E-Commerce Service Fee Support Program* of SR 800 million to support all stores by offering to pay the fees to service providers for 3 months,
- *Postpone the repayment of all financing products* for 3 months by banks without any additional costs or fees for Saudi employees.

Other SAMA measures included suspending freezing of bank accounts for 30 days to specific cases, raising E-Wallet top-up monthly ceiling limit up to SR 20,000 and postponing repayment of credit facilities (real estate, consumer and lease financing) for public and private health care workers for 3 months. While a lot of these measures are to alleviate short-term pain, the post COVID-19 period could also provide an opportunity for Saudi Arabia to be decisive and reset elements of the economy that have flagged and can capitalize on recent progress in the digital space.

4.2 FDI: Not Up to Expectations

Foreign Direct Investment (DFI) has been viewed in many countries as one of the key drivers for economic development as irrespective of their ideological differences, most countries around the world have been competing to attract FDI as there has been a sea change in the global economy precipitated by the phenomenon of globalization in recent decades (Saee 2005; Ramady and Saee 2007; Belloumi and Al Shehery 2018).

FDI can have both positive and some negative consequences, and some are listed below:

Positive factors:
- FDI can contribute to GDP, gross fixed capital formation and balance of payments, contribute towards debt servicing repayments, stimulate export markets and generate foreign exchange revenue,
- FDI can further stimulate product diversification through investments into new business,
- FDI can stimulate employment, raise wages, and replace declining market sectors,
- FDI can be a catalyst for infrastructure development and technology transfer.

Negative factors:
- Downside of FDI includes "crowding out" where FDI companies dominate local markets, stifling local competition and entrepreneurship, and "regulatory arbitrage" where government regulations, such as labor and environmental standards are kept artificially low to attract foreign investors. Lower standards can reduce the short-term operative costs in the country making FDI more attractive.

There are a variety of reasons why Saudi Arabia is encouraging FDI as part of its ambitious Vision 2030 program. There is a general consensus that the Kingdom truly needs to make economic reform work. It can only do so by strengthening the private sector, funding other sources of investment and encouraging repatriation of Saudi capital in viable domestic projects especially in projects unleashed in the Vision 2030 program such as the futuristic mega $500 billion *NEOM* ("New Future") City, as a hub for innovation, renewable energy and Artificial Intelligence application, creating opportunities for domestic and international technology cutting edge investors. In 2021, NEOM's vision was expanded further with the launch of the futuristic "The Line" – a city of 1 million residents, with a length of 170 km that preserves 95 % of nature within NEOM, with zero cars, zero streets, and zero carbon emissions (NEOM 2021).

In 2000, the Government of Saudi Arabia enacted the Foreign Investment Law and approved the formation of the Saudi Arabian General Investment Authority (SAGIA), with the aim for SAGIA to be a "one stop shop" authorized to issue licenses and incorporate new foreign and joint venture companies and cut through the then legendry red tape of Saudi bureaucracy (Ramady 2010). In this respect, SAGIA energetically embarked to establish a new operating framework that would be radically different from customary Saudi governmental departments with SAGIA having representatives from 16 government agencies at its disposal to speed up licensing decisions and approvals, with such approvals forthcoming in 30 days. This initial bold SAGIA initiative is set in Table 4.1 which summarizes the main changes in the 2000 Foreign Investment Law.

Table 4.1 Saudi Arabian Foreign Investment Law: comparison of Old and New Laws

Feature	New law	Previous law
Tax Holiday	• No reference is made to tax holidays and dividends taxes. This and many other details need to be clarified	• If Saudi share in company is greater or equal to 25%, foreign investors will not pay taxes during the first: - 10 years for industrial projects - 5 years for services and agricultural Projects
Taxing Scheme	• If the corporate profits of a company are less than SR100,000, they are taxed at the rate of 25%; the rate rises to 30% if corporate profits are more than SR100,000 - The new law reduced the tax brackets from four to only two	• If the corporate profits of a joint venture company are: - Less than SR100,000, the tax rate is 25% - More that SR100,000 but less than SR500,000, the tax rate is 35% - More than SR500,000 but less than R1,000,000, the tax rate is 40%. - More than SR1,000,000, the tax rate is 45%
Financial Losses	• No limitation on the number of future years that financial losses can be allocated to	• Financial losses can only be allocated to next year's operations
Loans from the Saudi Industrial Development Fund (SIDF)	• Companies fully or partially owned by foreigners can apply for subsidized loans from the SIDF.	• For company to apply for SIDF loans, the Saudi share in equity has to be at least 25%.
Ownership	• Full ownership of the project is granted to the licensed firm (including land, buildings, and housing for employees)	• There must be a Saudi partner/sponsor who would own the land
Sponsorship	• No Saudi sponsor is needed for the foreign investor. The licensed company will be the sponsor for the expatriate workers	• The Saudi partner will be the sponsor for the foreign investor and expatriates working in the joint venture company

Source: SAGIA

4.2 FDI: Not Up to Expectations

In essence, the new Foreign Investment Law gave foreign investors the same level of benefits, incentives, and guarantees offered to Saudi individuals and companies with the exception of the rate of taxation on profits, no limits on the number of years to carry forward financial losses, but the ability to obtain full concessionary Saudi financing from the Saudi Industrial Development Fund (SIDF). Something that had been a major obstacle to prospect FDI entrants, a 100% foreign ownership and self-sponsoring of company staff were approved. Further enhancements were made to the Foreign Investment Law to attract investments to the Kingdom, and in April 2003, the Saudi consultative council, the *Shoura,* decided to cut taxes on foreign companies' profits to 20% from the previous maximum of 30% levels and new legislation offered certain tax exemptions, especially for spending on research and development, but the discrepancy between foreign taxation at 20% and Saudi businesses who pay 2.5% zakat taxes remained (Ramady and Saee 2007).

Saudi Arabia had not been successful in attracting FDI levels to match the size of the economy. As comparison between 1984 and 1998, FDI to Saudi Arabia was $4.32 billion, compared with Singapore ($51.4 billion), Malaysia ($36 billion) and South Korea ($14.6 billion) prior to the Saudi 2000 Investment Law (World Bank 2020).

Figure 4.1 below sets out Saudi net FDI inflows over the period 1970–2019, and the picture is still erratic concerning FDI inflows, with the amount registered in 2019 ($4.563 billion) far below that for 2008 ($39.456 billion).

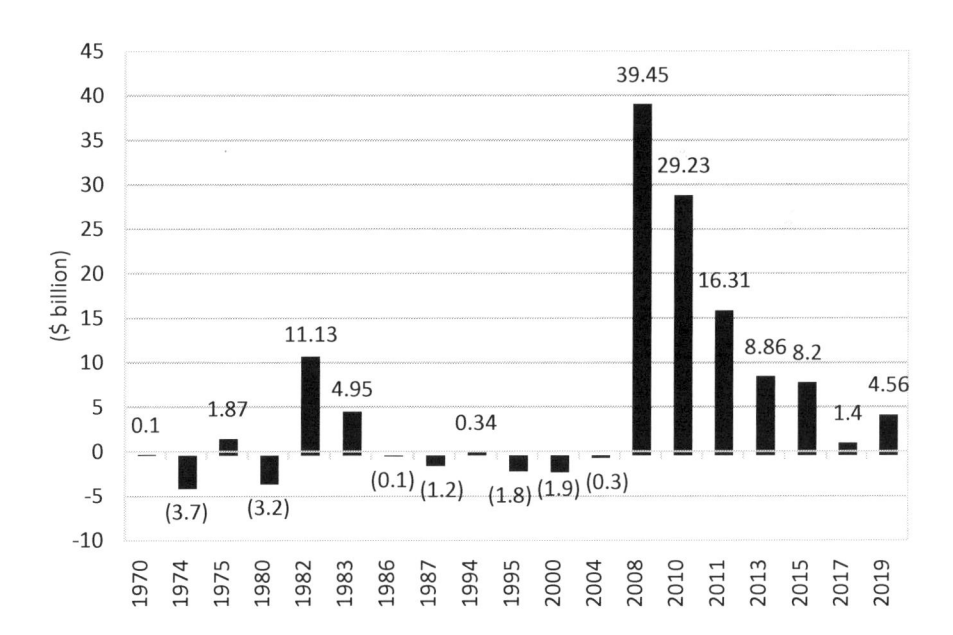

Source: World Bank, 2020.

Fig. 4.1 Saudi Arabian: net FDI inflows/outflows 1970–2019 ($ Billion). Source: World Bank (2020)

FDI inflows noted in Fig. 4.1 seemed to correlate with periods of regional geopolitical tensions, volatile, lower oil prices, showing marked increases in periods of higher oil prices with major inflows registered since 2008, but not reaching the FDI level registered since 2008. There are many reasons for this apparent lack of Saudi FDI success, such as conflicting signals on the policy of *Saudization* or imposing national labor quotas, foreign preference of a narrow base of FDI investment activities—mostly petrochemical related industries, and a fear of 'going it alone" without a local Saudi partner. FDI and the relationship between host countries and Multinational Companies (MNC's) has gone through various stages over the decades, depending on which partner felt they had the upper bargaining hand, as the question of balancing rights and responsibilities of MNC's and host state is important for an investment regime, and stability of international FDI investment regime. This is an ongoing struggle but Saudi Arabia seems to be approaching an equitable balance with MNC's as noted from the new 200 Investment Law. The announcement that the Kingdom plans to approve a set of new draft laws designed to enhance the efficiency and integrity of Saudi Arabia's judicial system in a step that would eventually lead to an entirely codified law is another reform to integrate Saudi Arabia in the modern legal system and encourage FDI (Rashad 2021).

Some suggestions have been made (Belloumi and Al Shehery 2018; Al Kathlan 2013) for a more effective and focused Saudi FDI program that includes the following:

- *Saudi Arabia should orient its domestic and foreign investments to more productive projects that can boost economic growth such as tourism and increase the participation of women in the labor force,*
- *Development of the Saudi military industries with foreign partners with more local content programs,*
- *Development of the mining sector as a new pillar of non-oil exports,*

The Saudi government has taken up the challenge to reinvigorate Saudi FDI inflows by appointing former Saudi energy minister and Aramco CEO Khalid Al Falih as Minister of Investments in 2020, with this new Ministry replacing SAGIA and in effect promoting SAGIA to a Ministerial position (Amlot 2020). As part of its new global liberalization and opening under the Vision 2030 program, the rebranding and empowering of SAGIA through the new Ministry of Investments bodes well, as Minister Al Falih is highly connected with international companies and potential investors from his earlier positions with Aramco and the Ministry of Energy, and having overseen mega FDI joint ventures in the Saudi energy sector.

The new Ministry of Investments has moved quickly to articulate its investment principles and policies and the range of investor support it is willing to extend to foreign FDI investors. In summary some of these are:

I. Investment Principles and Policies

- Ensure equality between Saudi and non-Saudi investors, and among non-Saudi investors,
- Ensure protection of investments

- Enhance the sustainability of investments and deal with investor complaints in a transparent manner,
- Provide investment incentives when needed and ensure full transparency when granting,
- Transfer and localize science and technology resulting from FDI

II. Investor Support

- *Market and economic intelligence*
  - Provide standard information packages
  - Provide periodic reports and case studies
  - Share contacts and data base
- *Matchmaking and linkage*
  - Industry/trade association commissions
  - Large local companies for potential partnerships
  - SME's for supply Chain Universities and research centers
- *Location search*
  - Connect with real estate agents for assistance and evaluation
- *Set up assistance*
  - Advice on corporate structure
  - Liaise with govt agencies to provide advice on visa applications, permits and licenses
  - Connect with recruiting employees agencies
  - Connect with financial partners for co-financing and support,
- *Incentives assistance*
  - Advise and develop specific incentive packages, and mediate disputes with local authorities
  - Build business case and feasibility studies
- *Improving business climate*
  - Develop policy recommendations based on feedback
  - Summit investors proposals for amendment of legislation
  - Troubleshoot investor operational issues

Reviewing these enhanced FDI investor services, one can conclude that the Kingdom has now adopted a more holistic management education process in the same way as any other successful developing country that fosters an enterprising corporate culture that is globally focused and cross-cultural savvy.

4.3 Vision 2030 Financial Plan: Adjustment in the Era of COVID 19

Looking back at what has been achieved so far concerning the implementation of the Vision 2030 program, especially its financial achievements, Saudi Crown Prince Mohammed bin Salman saluted the 'unprecedented' Saudi achievements made in increasing non-oil revenues, creating employment opportunities, especially for women and the anti-corruption campaign to tackle the previous "cancer" of rife corruption in the Kingdom (Arab News 2020a). While sometimes analysts focus on statistical data highlighting growth in certain indices such as investments, savings and GDP growth, it is also important to assess the sources of such growth, especially if it is concentrated in few hands and was achieved using so-called 'wasta' or 'connections' to obtain government projects through corrupt means, often adding higher costs to the general economy (Ramady 2016). The Saudi anti-corruption campaign initiated in 2017 under the auspices of the *NAZAHA* anti corruption body, has resulted in settlements amounting to SR 247 billion in 3 years according to the Crown Prince and reinforced the perception that no one is above the law concerning ongoing anti-corruption investigations. The Crown Prince listed other achievements whereby after investing more than SR 55 billion in digital infrastructure in the period 2017–2020, Saudi Arabia now ranks first among G20 members states in terms of digital competitiveness and has climbed 40 places on the Digital Infrastructure Index. Raising non-oil revenues was a central plank of the Vision 2030 program, noting that this had reached SR 360 billion in 2020 compared with SR 100 billion in 2015 and ensuring that public sector salaries were not curtailed, with expenditure of SR 188 billion expended to date on COVID-19 health care.

Besides the above COVID-19 initiative, the Saudi government took pro-active steps to support the financial sector, especially the SME sector, which included:

- A SR 30 billion deferred payment program for banks and financing companies to delay the payment of the dues of these entities from SME's for a period of 6 months,
- A SR 13.2 billion concessional financing program for SME's by granting loans from banks and finance companies to the SME sector to support business continuity and sector growth and maintaining employment levels to these enterprises,
- A SR 6 billion SME loan guarantee program to relieve SME's from the finance costs of the *KAFALA* program,
- A SR 800 million to support fees of POS—point of sales—and E-commerce payment of fees for all stores and entities in the private sector for a period of 3 months, with SAMA paying these fees.

Other Saudi government measures included allocation of SR 50 billion to accelerate payment dues form the government to the private sector, SR 43 billion for deferrals, exemptions for expat levies, postponing VAT, excise and personal income tax, postponing collection of customs duties and municipal fees, 50% discount on electricity bills for two months SR 9 billion private sector wage support, and SR 2 billion to provide support for 100,000 jobs seekers (NCB 2020).

The Financial Sector Development Plan (FSDP) is one of the twelve programs to achieve the Kingdom's 2030 Vision that was approved by the Council of Economic and Development Affairs (Jadwa 2019). For the Saudi finance sector, it is an important guideline going forward to implement a number of initiatives that fall under three main pillars:

4.3 Vision 2030 Financial Plan: Adjustment in the Era of COVID 19

(a) *Enabling financial institutions to support the growth of the private sector, previously examined in this book,*
(b) *Developing an advanced financial market, again explored in a previous chapter in this book,*
(c) *Promoting and enabling financial planning.*

To achieve the above, involves a close partnership between the main Saudi stakeholders—SAMA, the Ministry of Finance and the Capital Market Authority, something that has become apparent as we examined the roles of each player in the book. The FSDP program seeks to achieve five objectives, which are:

1. Financial diversity,
2. Financial inclusion
3. Financial stability,
4. Digital transformation
5. Depth of the financial market.

Figure 4.2 illustrates the 3 main pillars and the detailed 5 objectives, 2020 commitments and 2030 aspirations of the Vision 2030 program.

Pillars	2020 Commitments	2030 Aspirations
Enabling fin. institutions to support private sector	Financial assets/ GDP from 192 to 201 percent by 2020	Financial assets/ GDP large enough to fund all Vision 2030 objectives
Developing an advanced capital market	Capital markets assets from 41 to 45 percent by 2020 & introducing 3 financial technology players	Offering a diverse set of products and services through traditional (mortgages/ insurance) and newly emerging (fintech) players.
Promoting and enabling financial planning	Share of SME financing from 2 to 5 percent by 2020 & share of mortgages financing from 7 to 16 percent by 2020	Inclusive structure through higher bank account penetration and SME/ mortgage lending
	Increasing the share of non-cash transactions form 18 to 28 percent by 2020	More digitized economy including higher level of non-cash transactions
	Financial stability through compliance with international standards	Financial stability through compliance with international standards

Source: Vision 2030 FSDP Program

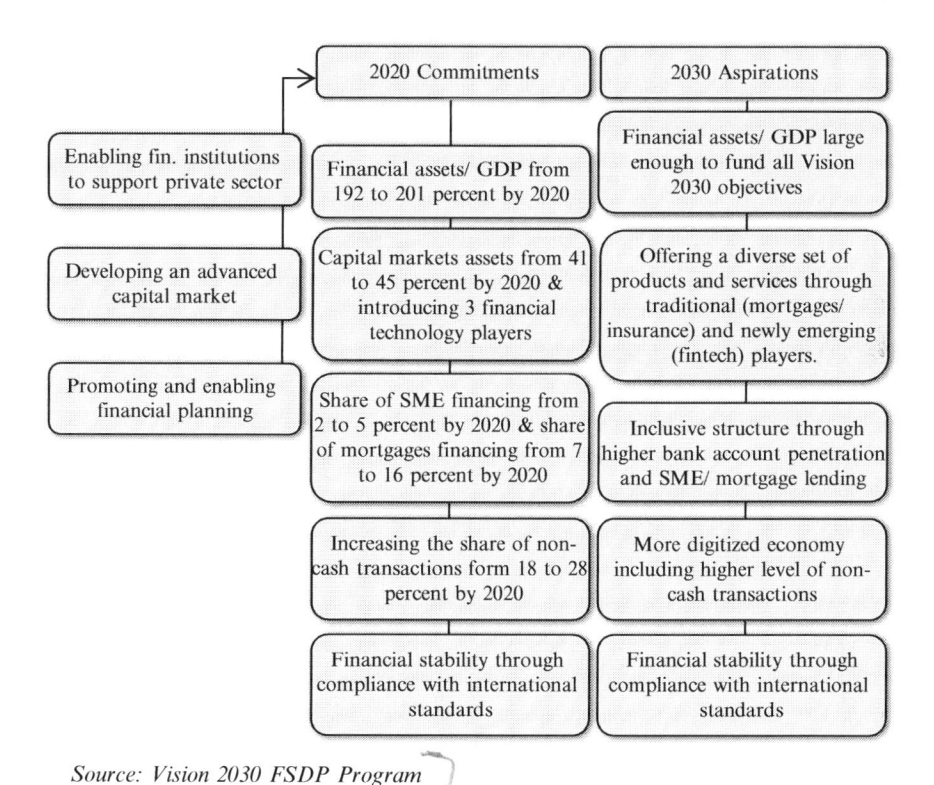

Fig. 4.2 The Saudi FSDP key Pillars, Commitments and Vision 2030 aspirations. Source: Vision 2030 FSDP Program

From Fig. 4.2, several 2020 commitments are introduced to align Saudi Arabia to either international best practices, or to be part of globalized financial sector trends. These are: opening the door of the financial services sector to emerging actors such as Fintech companies discussed previously in the book, so as to stimulate innovation and growth, and to being in full compliance with international standards related to financial stability, including the requirements of the Bank for International Settlements (BIS) and the International Organization of Securities Commission. The inclusion of the Saudi stock exchange *Tadawul* in leading global emerging market indices is a reflection of the appropriate high standard of the Saudi CMA regulators, and Saudi banks exceeding BIS Tier 2 and higher capitalization requirements also attests to Saudi over compliance of international standards under SAMA's stewardship.

Globalization however, also brings risks to the Saudi FSDP program, especially to Capital Market initiatives as well as to the overall financial market. These are:

- Inability to attract the best talent required by the financial sector,
- Other countries progressing faster in international indicators, especially global competitiveness indices that may affect the attractiveness of foreign investment to the Saudi Capital Market,
- Risks of financial technology innovation that may affect the efficiency of supervision of Saudi Arabia's Capital Market Authority,
- A possible high rate of failure of listed companies with the increasing issuance of both the main market and the parallel *NOMU* market, affecting investor confidence.

In summary, despite the 2020 COVID-19 pandemic, the Saudi Vision 2030 FSDP program has laid a firm foundation for wider domestic participation and international acceptance, by:

- Facilitating financing opportunities and strengthening the role of the financial market in providing sources of financing for the national economy,
- Stimulating investment by increasing domestic market attractiveness to investors and facilitating investment awareness,
- Enhancing confidence in developing the regulatory environment and raising levels of governance and transparency,
- Building the knowledge and technical capacities of market participants.

4.4 GCC Monetary Union: Unfinished Business

The Gulf Cooperation Council (GCC) is a regional integration formed in 1981 by the six Gulf countries—Saudi Arabia, Kuwait, UAE, Bahrain, Qatar and Oman— during the Iran-Iraq war, as a means of fostering Gulf security and economic interests (Ramady 2010). When the GCC was formed, the member countries aspired for a monetary union which is basically an economic union with a single common

4.4 GCC Monetary Union: Unfinished Business

currency, such as the Euro in the member countries of the European Union, but with some countries opting out of a common currency as was the case of the United Kingdom which continued to use its national currency, the pound sterling.

With the creation of the GCC in 1981, the member countries agreed to enhance cooperation between monetary agencies and central banks, including an aspiration to establish a common currency in order to further their desired economic integration (Shebab 2016). The Heads of State of the GCC decided at the end of 2001 in Oman to deepen this economic integration by establishing a common currency in 2010. A decade later this had not happened, leaving it as an unfinished business for the GCC.

The December 2001 Oman meeting had been optimistic about the eventual success for a common GCC currency union in that it would help to achieve a high level of harmonization in all economic fields—fiscal, monetary, banking and budgetary among the member states (Ramady 2010, 2014). As part of the economic agreement, the GCC countries launched the common market from the beginning of 2008, with no restriction on the mobility of goods, national labor (except those from sensitive security/defense background), and capital among the member countries that saw some members like the UAE benefit from GCC capital inflows, especially in the Dubai real estate and service sectors. They also agreed to eliminate all tariff and non-tariff barriers of intra-GCC trade and from 2003 started to treat any good as a national product as if it is produced by any GCC member state. A common tariff was introduced in 2003 that includes a common external customs tariff and common custom regulation.

But cracks began to appear along the way to establish a Gulf Monetary Union by 2010 as originally planned, as in 2007 Kuwait unilaterally moved from its U.S. dollar peg to an undisclosed currency basket and other GCC countries—Oman in 2006, and the UAE in 2009—pulled out of the proposed monetary union (Shebab 2016; Said 2018). While the withdrawal of the UAE from the project seems to have been due to a dispute with Saudi Arabia over the location of the future GCC central bank, which Saudi Arabia wanted located in Riyadh, the issue of the U.S. dollar and its peg to most of the Gulf countries is a key issue, given the centrality of a fixed SR peg to the dollar as examined in Chap. 1 of the book. The positive arguments for a single currency is that it leads to the elimination of transaction costs and uncertainties—monitoring exchange rates and predicting their fluctuations, costs of currency conversion, and keeping and managing reserves for intro-regional trade, but others argue that GCC countries like Kuwait have varying policies with the dollar peg and as such, monetary union for these countries takes away some of their autonomy (Said 2018).

Participating in a monetary union will undoubtedly involve losing autonomy over monetary instruments such as interest and exchange rates that serve as stabilizers, and monetary policies in one country impacts monetary policies in other countries which can in turn impact GDP growth and investments in countries that have unequal economic weight in a monetary bloc. Saudi Arabia is the dominant economic player in the GCC bloc and in a monetary union and common currency,

Saudi fiscal and monetary policy actions could affect smaller GCC economies, and hence Oman's withdrawal from the proposed monetary union.

Despite these setbacks, the GCC countries have sporadically continued discussions on the GCC monetary union, but in reality, the issue of sovereignty and autonomy makes this coming to reality a more distant proposition. The dispute between Qatar and other GCC member states—Saudi Arabia, UAE and Bahrain—which began in 2017, has also diminished prospects for a quick Gulf Monetary Union agreement, despite some indication from 2019 that some members of the GCC are trying to mitigate the effects of the dispute and stabilize relations with Qatar (Feierstein 2020). In January 2021, these efforts seem to have borne fruit with the boycotting Arab states agreeing to end their boycott of Qatar and restoring diplomatic relations during their 41st GCC Summit held at *Al Ula* in Saudi Arabia (Wintour 2021). The COVID-19 pandemic could bring the GCC countries together to face a common unseen enemy and coordinate on mutually beneficial health programs, but at the same time this could also put the aspiration for a common GCC currency to a backburner for some time, with Saudi Arabia focusing on a far more grander stage and global role such as its G20 Presidency and its role beyond its presidency of that body in 2020.

4.5　G20 Leadership: The Kingdom at Global Center Stage

On 21 and 22 November, 2020, the G20 summit concluded with Saudi Arabia acting as host after taking over the G20 presidency from Japan which hosted the 2019 G20 summit. The fact that the Saudi summit concluded on a virtual basis for the G20 leaders did not diminish the extraordinary efforts made by the host country during 2020 to tackle previous global issues as well as new ones thrown up by the COVID 19 global pandemic. The administration of the G20 presidency is no easy feat, even for advanced economies which had hosted the event, as more than 120 workshops, ministerial meetings and specialized seminars were scheduled in the Kingdom throughout 2020.

Riyadh's G20 summit was entrusted with the following three main focus areas:

- Empowering people
- Safeguarding the planet
- Shaping new frontiers

Figure 4.3 summarizes the main sub-tracks.

4.5 G20 Leadership: The Kingdom at Global Center Stage

Empowering people
- Unleashing Access to Opportunities for all by breaking barriers
- Boosting financial inclusion of women and youth
- Concrete action to finance the 2030 sustainable development agenda
- Promoting accessible, safe and person-centric health system
- Creating inclusive tourism destinations

Safeguarding the Planet
- Creating cleaner and more sustainable energy systems
- Focusing on energy access and the use of all energy sources
- Minimizing land degradation by reforesting the planet
- Improving global water management, and reducing global food loss

Shaping New Frontiers
- Utilizing technology in infrastructure
- Delivering a global solution to tax challenges from digitalization
- Developing smart cities and creating trustworthy artificial intelligence (AI)
- Harvesting the benefits from the entry of Big Tech in finance
- Tracking emerging risks, and ensuring cyber resilience

Source: Saudi G20 Secretariat, www.G20.org.

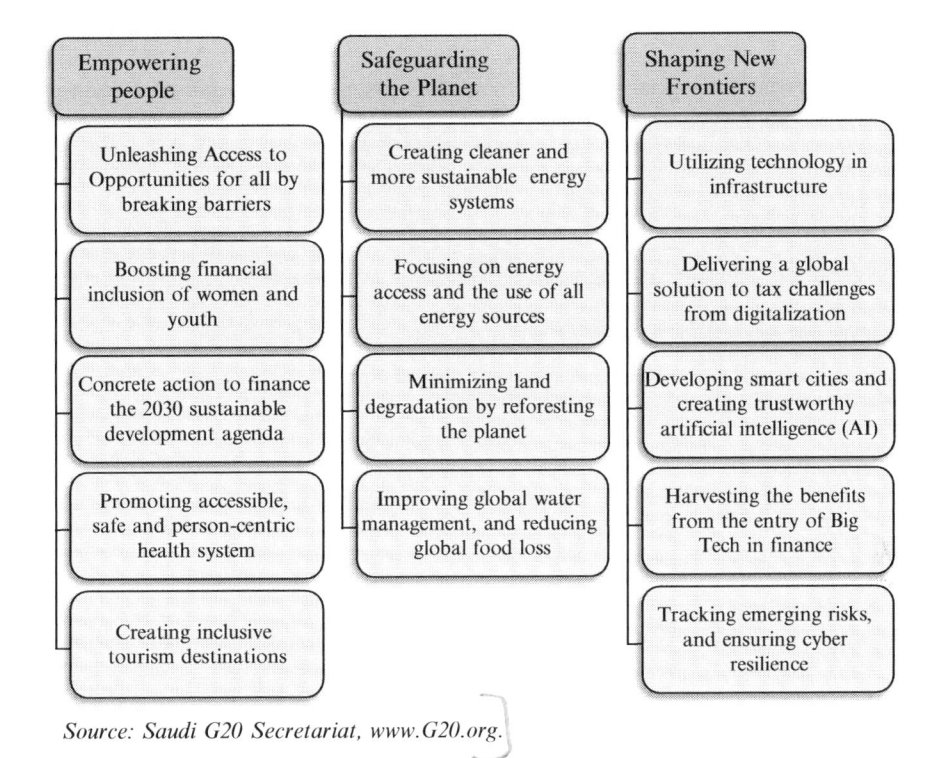

Fig. 4.3 Saudi G20 summit agenda: realizing opportunities of the twenty-first century for all. Source: Saudi G20 Secretariat (2020), www.G20.org

Adopting the G20's mission goal of *"Realizing Opportunities in the 21st Century for All"* was an adept one, with a collective roadmap focusing on the three pillars:

- *Empowering People:* The G20 aimed to create the conditions in which all people can live, work and thrive to empower both women and youth, encourage quality jobs, promote education and skills and scale-up efforts for sustainable developments,
- *Safeguarding the Planet:* Advancing synergies between adaptation and mitigation efforts to tackle climate change, protecting the environment, promoting clearer and more sustainable energy systems and affordable energy access,
- *Shaping New Frontiers:* Utilizing and sharing the benefits of innovation through international collaboration and harnessing the benefits of digitalization across economies, including advances in Artificial Intelligence and development of 'Smart Cities'.

The G20 Presidency established various engagement groups comprised of independent stakeholders from international experts, which gave a chance to many Saudi experts to participate and acquire relevant skills. Figure 4.4 illustrates the various G20 tracks and sub-tracks.

Financial Track	Global economy	International finance architecture
	Infrastructure	International taxation
	Financial regulation	Financial inclusion

Sherpa Track	Agriculture	Education	Health
	Anti-corruption	Employment	Tourism
	Climate change	Energy	Trade & Investment
	Digital Economy	Environment	

Engagement Groups	Business	Civil	Think
	Youth	Women	Urban
	Labor	Science	

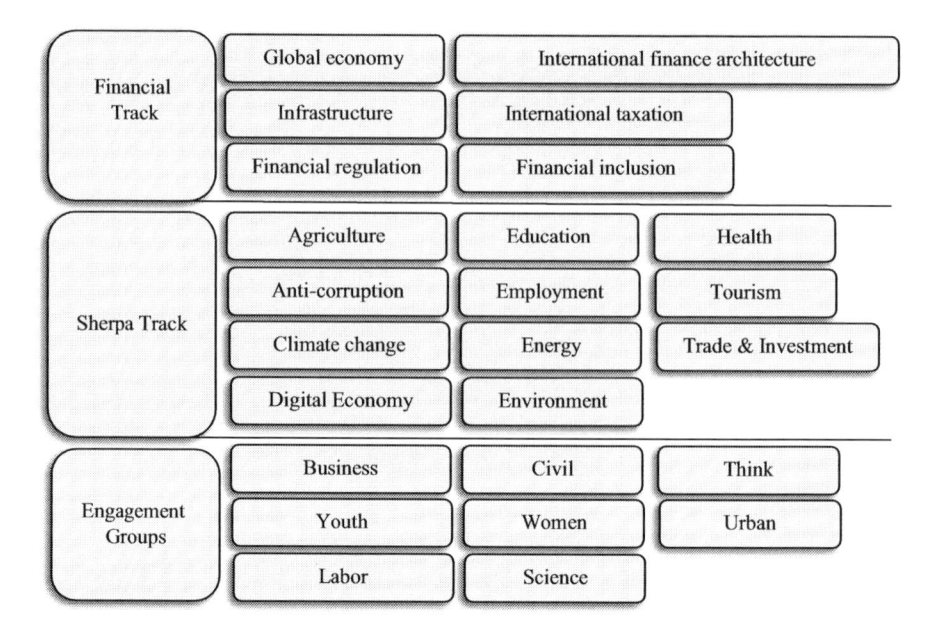

Source: G20 Secretariat, Riyadh

Fig. 4.4 G20 specialist tracks and sub-tracks. Source: G20 Secretariat, Riyadh

The various tracks and their focus areas were:

1. ***The Finance Track:*** this includes meetings of the G20 finance ministers and central bank governors and their deputies. For Saudi Arabia Finance Minister Al Jadaan and former SAMA governor Al Kholifey played an active role, not only focused on fiscal and monetary policy issues but also on cross-border payments and in cooperation with the Bank for International Settlements Innovation Hub, launched the G20 TechSprint Initiative to highlight the potential for new technologies to resolve regulatory compliance (Reg Tech) and supervision (Sup Tech) challenges.
2. ***The Sherpa Track:*** this includes meetings of ministers and relevant senior officials from government entities that focus on socio-economic issues. By all accounts, specialized Saudi entities like KAPSARC—King Abdullah Petroleum Studies and Research Center—took initiatives on the environment and climate change program.
3. ***Engagement groups:*** this represented civil society groups, with representatives of the business community, women, youth, labor and think tanks. By all accounts, the issue of youth and women employment dominated the agenda of the L20 workers communications group meetings as a top priority. Given the young age profile of Saudi society where nearly 70% of the population is under 35 years, and the encouragement of women's participation in all aspects of Saudi Arabia's life under the Vision 2030 program, this focus was not surprising.

4.5 G20 Leadership: The Kingdom at Global Center Stage

As noted earlier, many Saudi stakeholders took part in the engagement groups. Table 4.2 explores this further and sets out the leading Saudi Arabian leading organizations taking part with virtually all Saudi universities also taking part.

Table 4.2 G20 Engagement groups and Saudi leading organizations.

Engagement groups	Objectives	Leading organizations
B20: Business 20	Represents the global business community across all G20 countries, and provides specific policy recommendations by the private sector	Council of Saudi Chambers
Y20: Youth 20	Brings together young leaders from across the G20 members	Misk & Ithraa
L20: Labor 20	Represents the interests of workers around the world, and promotes and advocate for workers' rights	Saudi National Committee for Labor Committees
T20: Think 20	A network of think tanks and researchers, providing research-based policy recommendations	King Abdullah Petroleum Studies & Research Center (KAPSARC) and King Faisal Center for Research & Islamic Studies (KFCRIS)
C20: Civil Society 20	Provides a platform for civil society organizations around the world to contribute to the G20 agenda	King Khalid Foundation (KKF)
W20: Women 20	Aims to ensure that the gender considerations are mainstreamed into G20 discussions	Al-Nahdha Organization
S20: Science 20	Allows science academies to effectively contribute to the G20 by capturing non-governmental, non-business voices of the scientific community	King Abdullah University of Science & Technology (KAUST)
U20: Urban 20	Aims to bring sustainable urban development issues to the forefront of the G20 agenda	Royal Commission for Riyadh City

Source: Jadwa Investment (2020b)

The inclusion of leading Saudi organizations noted in Table 4.2 is important in many respects as the Saudi participants are not only expanding their technical skills but also making new friendships and networking contacts for future cooperation on mutual issues of concern. The G20 Presidency has provided a generation of future Saudi leaders with international exposure.

Under Saudi Arabia's G20 Presidency, the country has also ensured that other non-G20 members and international organizations were invited to attend, in addition to the G20 members. Spain is a permanent guest invitee to the G20 meetings. In 2020, Jordan, Singapore and Switzerland were invited as guest countries. International Organizations that have historically contributed to the G20 work were invited as well. These include the Food and Agriculture Organization (FAO), the Financial Stability Board (FSB), the International Labor Organization (ILO), the

International Monetary Fund (IMF), the Organization for Economic Cooperation and Development (OECD), the United Nations (UN), the World Bank Group (WBG), the World Health Organization (WHO) and the World Trade Organization (WTO).

In 2020, regional organizations were also invited, including the Arab Monetary Fund (AMF), the Islamic Development Bank (IsDB), as well as Vietnam, the Chair of the Association of Southeast Asian Nations (ASEAN), South Africa, the Chair of the African Union (AU), the United Arab Emirates, the Chair of the Gulf Cooperation Council (GCC), and the Republic of Rwanda, the Chair of the New Partnership for Africa's Development (NEPAD). All the above initiatives have added depth to the G20's global outreach to avoid giving the impression that it is an exclusive club.

During the G20 presidency, Saudi Arabia played an active role in the finance track, especially in contributing in the fight against the COVID-19 pandemic effects on poorer nations, especially on debt relief (Cronin 2020; Reuters 2020b). A comprehensive Debt Service Suspension Initiative was agreed for 73 countries, with the aim to building a long-term transparent and inclusive system for cancelling debts to a sustainable level across private, bilateral and multilateral lenders.

The International Financial Architecture task force was an important one for Saudi Arabia's financial regulators as it focused on global financial governance, and cooperation between multinational and regional authorities to manage financial stability and discuss encouraging inclusive financial sector development via new instruments, including the role of Islamic finance. As noted earlier in this book, the Saudi financial sector is served by institutions that are fully *Shariah* compliant as well as institutions that are 'mixed' or also offer Islamic finance products and the popularity of this finance sector has been growing globally and in the Kingdom, including the issuance of *Sukuk* bonds and other financial instruments by the Saudi government (Mahrotra, Miyajima and Villar 2012).

Other finance task force priorities examined, included:

- *Global risks and crisis in capital flow and international institutions,*
- *Governing and regulating crypto currency and Fintech, and their impact on the international monetary system,*
- *Global financial governance and central bank independence,*
- *Global financial monitoring of money laundering, terror financing and the efficiency of financial institutions.*

As noted in Chaps. 1 and 2, SAMA has been proactive in many of the above task force priorities, especially in monitoring of money laundering and financial institution governance, and the G20 presidency added to Saudi governance skills, especially addressing potential risks to the financial system from cyber incidents and the use of technology in regulation. The Saudi government and its financial regulators have also not been shy to take decisive measures to combat financial corruption with the capital Market Authority referring 22 investors to the Public Prosecution Office over suspicious trading in shares and making illicit gains of SR 1.33 billion (Argaam 2020c), and the Saudi Control and Anti Corruption Authority *NAZAHA* launching more than 150 criminal investigations (Arab News 2020b). The message is clear: no one is above the law and investor's rights are safeguarded, whether local or national.

4.5 G20 Leadership: The Kingdom at Global Center Stage

According to the World Competitiveness Yearbook (WCY), Saudi Arabia is ranked second globally in the field of corporate cyber security and jumped nine places to become number 12 among the G20 countries in the e-government development index, reflecting the achievements of the Vision 2030 program, and according to the WCY, Saudi Arabia ranked 7th globally in financing technical developments (Saudi Gazette 2020). Such achievements to be part of global developments and lead in other areas have not come overnight, but through a comprehensive and proactive regulatory framework.

The importance and urgency of climate action and delivering on the Paris Climate Agreement to reduce emissions and transition away from fossil fuel-based technologies was highlighted in the Sherpa environment track (Fig. 4.4). The S20 (Science 20) circular economy task force took the initiative on this holistic 'cradle-to-grave" valuation of the social, economic and environmental dimensions of resource utilization and waste production/ reduction.

The concept of a 'circular carbon economy' is an area where Saudi Arabia not only excelled but also has led the way amongst the major oil producers. The concept of a 'circular carbon economy' has been the proponent of Saudi Energy Minister Prince Abdul-Aziz bin Salman even before the G20 presidency when he announced a "closed loop system" which will help restore carbon balance and contribute to global economic growth in a sustainable manner. According to the Prince, carbon is not the enemy, but that with a circular carbon economy, carbon can be an opportunity. In summary, the concept of a circular carbon economy offers a new way of approaching climate goals that implicitly values all options and encourages all efforts to mitigate carbon accumulation in the atmosphere. The circular carbon economy differs from the concept of a circular economy in that it focuses exclusively on carbon and energy flows and is characterized by the four 'R's':

1. ***Reduce***
   'Reduce' represents all of the carbon mitigation options that reduce the amount of carbon entering the system. Energy efficiency, both on the supply and demand side, reduces energy consumption and the associated carbon. Similarly, energy supply options that do not emit carbon, such as non-biomass renewables and nuclear power, also reduce the flow of carbon into the system, though they can indirectly result in carbon emissions during their manufacture, construction, and installation.

2. ***Reuse***
   In the context of the circular carbon economy, 'reuse' refers to capturing and using carbon as an input to a chemical or industrial process that converts the carbon to another useful feedstock for industry. Carbon utilization fits squarely within the tradition of industrial ecology by 'metabolizing' carbon from a waste to a valuable input. For example, the Saudi Arabian Basic Industries Corporation (SABIC) utilizes its own carbon dioxide (CO_2) waste in the world's largest carbon capture and utilization plant

3. ***Recycle***
   'Recycle' represents the natural carbon cycle, in which natural sinks (e.g., plants, soil and oceans) draw carbon from the atmosphere and then release it again

through decomposition and combustion. The carbon is effectively recycled, and the bio-energy subsystem can be considered carbon neutral, as long as an equal amount of biomass grows to replace what is harvested as bio-feedstock (e.g., wood, fuel crops, algae, etc.) for bioenergy.

4. **Remove**

The final 'R' of the circular carbon economy represents the removal of carbon from the system. Captured carbon can be either converted to feedstock, as discussed above in 'reuse,' or removed by storing it geologically or chemically. Carbon can be captured directly from industrial processes and points of combustion, but it can also be captured directly from the air with direct air capture.

With such a bold new vision for addressing climate change, Saudi Arabia had an exceptional opportunity to shift the climate debate during its G20 presidency and in the wider international community, as Saudi Arabia is fully aware that in the foreseeable future the global path towards a carbon balance will inevitably include fossil fuels, but that their carbon emissions must be mitigated.

To add to its cutting-edge technology in the field of circular carbon economy, the Kingdom has successfully demonstrated the production and shipment of the world's first *'blue ammonia'* to Japan in September 2020 (Saudi Aramco 2020). According to Aramco, some 40 tons of high-grade blue ammonia for use in ZERO CARBON power generation in Japan, signaled the role that hydrogen will play in the global energy system. Ammonia is a compound consisting of three parts hydrogen and one-part nitrogen and the blue ammonia supply network demonstration spanned the full value chain, which also included the capture of associated carbon dioxide (CO_2) emissions. Apparently, some 30 tons of CO_2 was captured during the process designated to use in methanol production at SABIC's *Ibn-Sina* facility and another 20 tons of captured CO_2 used for Enhanced Oil Recovery at Aramco's *Uthmaniyah* oil field (Saudi Aramco 2020). This breakthrough puts the Kingdom as a true global leader in the reduced, removed, recycled and reused circular carbon economy ensuring its place in a globalized climate conscious world.

During the G20 concluding statements, King Salman of Saudi Arabia announced that the Kingdom will launch the national program of circular carbon economy and highlighted the world's largest carbon capturing facility established by SABIC with a total capacity of 500,000 tons annually, and of Saudi Aramco's plan for improved oil exploration with a total capacity of 800,000 tons of captured carbon emission annually.

In summary the 2020 G20 summit in Riyadh and the Presidency of the event by the Kingdom, the first even G20 meeting held in the Arab world, has brought into focus the challenges faced by countries in the Middle East. Substantive issues such as attracting investment, sustainable energy, and reforming labor market and creating opportunities for a largely youthful population and women participation have been debated and Saudi Arabia is keen to implement the G20 leader's final recommendations.

4.6 Conclusion

Analysis of the Saudi financial structure and its main regulators, SAMA and the Capital Market Authority, has illustrated the significant progress made over the past few decades to oversee a multi-faceted financial sector. The regulatory emphasis has erred on the conservative side with pragmatism, stability and continuity being the watchword, especially for SAMA. Under various governors, SAMA has survived and come out stronger since its creation throughout a range of crisis that would have put other regulators under severe pressure, with some governors like one of the world's longest serving central bank governors *Hamad Al Sayari*, with 35 years of SAMA stewardship in managing the institution over multiple turbulent domestic and regional crisis cycles. The newly reappointed 2021 SAMA governor Dr. Fahad Al Mubarak, who was SAMA Governor from 2011–2016 (Arab News 2021) will continue with his predecessors pragmatism and continuity while meeting the challenges of digital and FinTech banking, regulating a new wave of foreign banks and overseeing mega Saudi bank mergers. Asset quality and liquidity in the Saudi financial sector are now well established through a balanced SAMA regulatory oversight installing sound banking practices, through strong capitalization, high credit quality and healthy profitability for the sector. Overlapping areas of supervisory jurisdiction of investment banking and financial instruments has been resolved between SAMA and a mature and confident Capital Market Authority that has come of age in terms of depth and multiplicity of players.

In a development that could reinforce the current power and mandate of SAMA, the Saudi *Shoura* Consultative Council endorsed a draft Saudi Central Bank Act during its regular session held on 16 November 2020 which was passed into Law by Saudi King Salman bin Abdul Aziz on 24 November 2020 (Argaam 2020a; Saudi Press Agency 2020; SAMA 2020). According to the *Shoura* Council's Finance Committee head Mr. Saleh Al Khelawi, the new Act rebrands SAMA as the Saudi Central Bank in line with central banks in other countries and enhances SAMA's monitoring as well as supervision capacities by granting the Saudi Central Bank more independence and flexibility in managing foreign investments. The rebranded SAMA as a central bank—which according to SAMA will still use the acronym SAMA due to its historical relevancy—will enter a new phase since its establishment in 1952, confident that it has built a strong foundation for the new challenges it faces, especially if the new central bank pursues a higher yield seeking investment objective compared to the current conservative approach to ensure coverage of the Saudi Riyal as discussed in Chap. 1. This will raise some interesting questions on whether the new Saudi Central Bank will still focus on monetary investments as opposed to investment in corporate equities like the Public Investment Fund. From the Press release announcing the new Central Bank , it is more than likely that the new Central Bank will continue in its primary mission in managing monetary policy and reserves and supervising the financial sector 's institutions , including banks , finance companies , insurance companies , the credit information sector and the Fin Tech sector (SAMA 2020).

The Saudi financial sector has also benefited from the cross fertilization of skills and experience of senior financial executives who have taken on new roles as regulators and thus are familiar with their regulatory counterparts thinking and planned regulatory programs. Amongst those that come to mind who have shaped and are shaping current financial policies by bringing with them multi-faceted financial sector experience are *Yasser Al Rumayyan* (Secretary General of the PIF and former CEO of Saudi Fransi Capital and current CMA Board member), *Dr.Fahad Al Mubarak* (reappointed SAMA Governor and former MD of Morgan Stanley, and Chairman of *Tadawul*), *Jamaz Al Suhaimi* (until his death in 2017 was Director General of SAMA Banking Control Department and Secretary General of the CMA, as well as Chairman of Gulf International Bank), *Mohammed Al Jadaan* (current Minister of Finance and Economy who was special Advisor to Morgan Stanley and Chairman of the CMA), *Mohammed El Kuwaiz* (current Chairman of the CMA and former SAMBA executive and McKinsey and Co-founder of Derayah Finance Company), *Sarah Suhaimi* (CEO and Board Director of NCB Capital and current first female chair of *Tadawu*l), *Tareq Al Sadhan*, CEO of Riyad Bank and former Deputy Governor SAMA Bank Supervision, and *Mohammed Al Tuwaijri* (current Advisor to the Royal Court and former Minister of Economy as well as senior executive with HSBC and CEO of JP Morgan Saudi Arabia). Some SAMA governors also brought invaluable international multilateral experience from bodies such as the IMF and the BIS like *Dr. Mohammed Al Jasser* and former Governor *Dr. Ahmed Al Kholifey* . Others include *Jamal Rammah*, former Vice Chairman Riyad Bank and current Board Member, who was Aramco's Treasurer.

Such a rich and varied professional skill base, including many in middle management positions, has helped the Saudi financial sector to adopt best practice applications and groom a new generation of capable Saudi financial regulators with a strong commitment to ethical practices, for in the end, however, strong a bank's capital base or well written its compliance manual, it is an ethical underpinning that is more important for public confidence and sustainability of the sector. The Saudi financial sector should be proud of what has been achieved without major regulatory scandals compared with what was revealed in a mature western financial sector in the UK. A BBC investigative program into leaked documents—the Fin CEN Files—revealed that about $2 trillion of transactions have been allowed to be money laundered by some of the world's biggest banks where there was a grey line between banks reporting concerns about what their clients might be doing and reporting these to the U.S.A.'s Financial Crimes Enforcement Network or Fin CEN as opposed to acting upon these suspicions because of the profitability of their client relationship. Once a bank has filed a report to the authorities it is very difficult to prosecute it or its executives, even if it carries on helping with the suspicious activities and collecting fees (BBC 2020). The leaks have led to both the Fin CEN and the UK regulators to overhaul their anti-money laundering programs and reform the register of company information.

To its credit, SAMA's insistence on strict anti-money laundering regulations and oversight has played a major role in ensuring that the Saudi financial sector remains 'clean' despite protestations that SAMA is too excessive in its regulatory approach.

4.6 Conclusion

While SAMA is to be applauded for this tough regulatory stance Central Bank still finds itself faced by the following challenges in a post COVID-19 world:

- *Saudi Arabia is an open economy with no restrictions on capital flows, which makes capital control policies ineffective.*
- *The bulk of economic activity and revenues are oil-driven, and SAMA has not much control as to government inflows economic openness and oil dependency means vulnerability to external shocks.*
- *A fixed exchange rate regime against the US dollar, which hampers SAMA's independent interest rate policies.*
- *A passive player in terms of the government's macroeconomic objectives of minimizing the impact of oil revenue swings though government-induced countercyclical measures, involving building surpluses in upswings and running deficits in downturns*

Assessing the above challenges, SAMA has affirmed its commitment to its exchange rate policy of pegging the Saudi Riyal to the U.S. dollar as a strategic choice that underpins economic growth and stability in Saudi Arabia. In our view, under the new Saudi Central Bank, risks to the Saudi Riyal peg will remain contained and that the Saudi authorities will remain committed to maintaining the peg. The most likely circumstances in which there is a possibility of a change in the foreign exchange regime would be if external balance sheets were to weaken to the point that they could no longer support the currency at current levels, which is unlikely in the medium term given the current high level of SAMA's reserves at $447 billion in September 2020, albeit significantly down from a peak of $732 billion end of 2014. A possibility to maintain the current peg is for the new Saudi Central Bank to introduce capital controls on outward flows, but the likelihood that this materializes is extremely remote given the Vision 2030 objectives of encouraging FDI inflows and supporting private sector non-oil GDP contribution. Saudi Arabia will continue to be an open, globalized economy for the foreseeable future. While Saudi Arabia encourages financial innovation and FinTech applications, the government has made it clear against dealing or investing in virtual currencies including crypto currencies as these are not recognized by legal entities in the Kingdom and are outside the scope of the regulatory framework and are not traded by financial institutions locally. The Saudi authorities have warned the public against using such virtual currencies marketing using Saudi Arabia national symbols or names such as Crypto Riyal otherwise they will be subject to legal actions.

Both COVID-19 and the collapse in global oil prices have had an impact on the GCC countries' external balances, but it is oil price volatility that is more important over the medium term for Saudi Arabia, given that despite significant improvement in non-oil revenues, oil exports still account for the majority of Saudi government revenues, accounting for two thirds of the Kingdom's exports. While oil prices are ranging between $ 58–61 a barrel as of mid-February 2021 these are still well below a level of $77 a barrel that the Kingdom needs to balance its budget according to the International Monetary Fund. Ensuring price stability and compliance with agreed production quotas by the so-called OPEC+ members is now an urgent strategic energy policy for Saudi Arabia, as it is the *de-facto* leader of the OPEC producers while Russia is the *de-facto* leader of the non-OPEC members in the group. The OPEC Secretariat is fully aware that consensus on compliance and adherence to production cuts is important for oil price, and hence, revenue stability in the face of demand destruction because of COVID-19 in the short-term, and 'peak oil' demand in the longer term due to climate change concerns and switch to renewables and cleaner energy sources. The successful initial trials of various anti-COVID vaccines in November 2020 lifted oil prices in early 2021 but remains at the mercy of fluctuating market enthusiasm once it was recognized that a global economy re-opening leading to increased energy demand might not materialize in the near term.

The importance for maintaining oil price stability was underscored by the dramatic collapse in oil prices during March and April 2020, when on 20 April, the price of West Texas Intermediate (WTI) oil price for May delivery fell into negative territory at $37 a barrel for the first time in history due to depressed demand and insufficient storage capacity, with producers forced to pay buyers to dispose of excess oil on the market (Ambrose 2020). The effects of this shock, which was initiated by Saudi Arabia increasing its production form 9.7 million barrels per day to 12.3 million barrels per day following disagreements with Russia, was felt in falls in world stock markets. Stability was restored only after the two de-factor leaders agreed to a reduction of 10 million barrels per day amongst members and laid out a long-term 2-year road map to manage individual production quotas, with the Kingdom taking the lead to making substantial production cuts over and above its agreed pact quotas to help oil price stability in Q1 2021.

Such erratic oil revenue dependency has forced Saudi Arabia to expand its domestic and international debt program, mostly the latter as examined in this book, along with its implication for its future debt servicing burden. According to some estimated forecasts (JP Morgan 2020), total Saudi external debt would reach $261.1 billion by year-end 2021, representing around 35.0% of GDP, while total government debt would reach $274.5 billion or 36.8% of GDP. At the same time, Saudi Arabia's international reserves would fall further to $369.9 billion by year end 2021.These are somewhat pessimistic forecasts and do not take into account a positive effect on global economic activity due to an accelerated effective anti-COVID-19 vaccine rollout, higher oil prices, and other non-oil revenue measures and expenditure rationalization programs introduced by Saudi Arabia to reduce government outlays. While some GCC countries are planning to introduce income tax on high earners by 2022, such as Oman which highlighted this in its latest 2020–2024 economic plan (Reuters 2020a), Saudi Arabia is not expected to follow suit given the rise in VAT rates from 5% to 15% in 2020 but which was waived on real estate transactions as noted in this book. With renewed emphasis in attracting FDI and foreign enterprises in the varied Vision 2030 programs, especially in entertainment and tourism, and NEOM, the likelihood of imposing income tax becomes less viable.

However, while the government itself is borrowing on the international markets, other Saudi entities, especially Saudi Aramco, have also tapped the international capital market with the latest being a $8 billion jumbo five part bond in November

4.6 Conclusion

2020 which received $48.1 billion in orders, half what Aramco drew for its debut bond sale in 2019 when it raised $12 billion, but still indicating strong global interest due to attractive yields offered (Saba 2020; MEE 2020). The latest Aramco bond tranches were in the three-year tenor (at 110 basis points over U.S. Treasuries, 5-year bonds (at 125 basis points), 10-year notes (at 145 basis points), 30-year bonds (3.3% over U.S. Treasuries), and a 50 Year Tranche at 3.55% yield. The 50-year tranche is the longest-dated international debt issued by Saudi Arabia as in April 2020 the government issued a 40-year bond tranche; at the time the longest dated dollar issuance by a Gulf borrower, only to be overtaken by Abu Dhabi with a 50-year tranche in August 2020. As with the previous bond and Aramco's $10 billion loan raised in 2020 to be repaid in installments until 2028, a who's who of blue chip international and selected Gulf banks were involved in the deal (Saba 2020). The COVID-19 and reduced oil prices have put under pressure the energy giant's capital expenditure programs and its commitment to maintain its $75 billion dividend policy, as well as its $69.1 purchase of 70% of Saudi Basic Industries (SABIC) from the Public Investment Fund. The international loans and bond issuances will assist Saudi Aramco meet its obligations on both counts and maintain confidence in Aramco ability to meet its commitments (MEE 2020). Cognizant of the large foreign debt holding, the Saudi Finance Minister noted in a Bloomberg interview on 20 November that Saudi Arabia is not planning to tap international debt markets again in 2020, as the Kingdom prefers local borrowing to fund the budget deficit as it has also borrowed SR 45 billion more than needed from domestic lenders and will use that over financing to help plug the rest of the 2020 deficit (Gamal El Din and Nereim 2020). However as noted earlier, the PIF has indicated that it might soon turn to the international debt market for a tranche of up to $15 billion in 2021, more than double what it sought in 2020, to raise funds for its growing domestic and international asset acquisitions and new mega projects (Martin and Narayanan 2021).

As discussed, Saudi Arabia's presidency of the G20 will long be remembered, not simply because it was held during an extraordinary COVID-19 pandemic year, but in the professional management of the year long event and the wide scale participation of many Saudi stakeholders. The results have been felt in several ways: *first*, the Kingdom has firmly established itself as the only Arab country among G20 members that carried the aspirations, not only of Saudi Arabia but of the wider Arab world; *second*, the Kingdom has emerged from the shadows to play a prominent global role at the center stage in helping to shape new frameworks in the international order to overcome global economic crisis. As Saudi government officials aptly put it, the G20 and its presidency has been called on to save the world, and to mitigate the effects of the crisis and ensured that global problems required global solutions, especially in ensuring equitable access to vaccination stock to poorer countries and support for the World Health Organization. *Thirdly,* the Kingdom has demonstrated its capability to host such a large-scale international event, that was not a one day event, but a full one year program, that show cased the Kingdom's advancement in infrastructure and also the competence and skills of its government and private sector participants to launch the Kingdom as a true global partner.

References

Al Kathlan, K. (2013). Foreign direct investment inflows and economic growth in Saudi Arabia: A C-integration analysis. *Review of Economic and Finance, 5*, 70–80.

Ambrose, J. (2020). Oil prices dip below zero as producers forced to pay to dispose of excess. *The Guardian,* Retrieved April 20, 2020, from www.theguardian.com

Amlot, M. (2020). *Meet Khalid Al Falih, Again Now as Saudi Minister of Investment.* Retrieved February 27, 2020, from www.Alrabiya.net

Arab News. (2020a). *Crown prince salutes unpresented Saudi achievements.* Arab News, November 13, 2020, from www.arabnews.com

Arab News. (2020b). *Saudi Control and Anti-Corruption Authority launches dozens of criminal cases.* Retrieved November 26, 2020, from www.arabnews.com

Arab News. (2021). *King Salman issues Royal Decrees.* Retrieved January 24, 2021. Arab News from www.arabnews.com

Argaam. (2020a). Central Bank Act allow SAMA more independence flexibility. *Argaam,* Retrieved November 17, 2020, from www.argaam.com

Argaam. (2020b). *NCB, SAMBA enter into legally binding merger agreement.* Retrieved October 11, 2020, from www.argaam.com

Argaam (2020c) *CMA refers 22 investors to public prosecution over suspicious trading in Dar Al Arkaan , illicit gains of SR 1.3 Bn.* Retrieved November 30, 2020, from www.argaam.com

BBC. (2020). Fin CEN Files: All you need to know about the document leak. *BBC Panorama,* Retrieved September 21, 2020, from www.bbc.com

Belloumi, M., & Al Shehery, A. (2018). The impacts of domestic and Foreign Direct Investment on Economic Growth in Saudi Arabia. *MDPI Economies, 6*(18) www.mdpi.com.

Cronin, S. (2020). *G20 finance chiefs back measures to Fight COVID-19 pandemic in poorest nations.* Retrieved November 13, 2020, from www.arabnews.com

Feierstein, G. (2020). *Three years on, the intra GCC dispute has taken a back seat but persists.* Washington, DC: Middle East Institute.

G20. (2020). Official website. from www.G20.org

Gamal El Din, Y. & Nereim, V. (2020). *Saudi Arabia wont tap Debt Market again in 2020.* Minister says Bloomberg.

J P Morgan. (2020). Emerging markets debts and fiscal indicators-2020. *Argaam,* Retrieved November 2020. www.jpmorgan.com

Jadwa Investment. (2019). *Update on the financial sector development plan.* Jada Investment. Retrieved September, 2019, from www.jadwa.com

Jadwa Investment. (2020a). *Saudi labor market update.* Jadwa Investment. Retrieved October 2020, from www.jadwa.com

Jadwa Investment. (2020b). *G20 in Saudi Arabia.* Jadwa Investment. Retrieved January, from www.jadwa.com

Mahrotra, A., Miyajima, K., & Villar, A. (2012). Development of government bond, markets in emerging market economies and their implications. In *Fiscal policy, public debt and monetary policy in emerging market economies.* BIS Papers 67.

Martin. M and Narayanan, A. (2021). *Saudi Wealth Fund may double loan to $ 15 billion for deals.* February 02, 2021. Bloomberg. www.bloomberg.com

MEE. (2020). *Saudi Aramco forced to sell billions of dollars in bonds to maintain $75 billion dividend.* Middle East Energy. from www.middleeast-energy.com.

NCB. (2020). *Saudi government response measures to COVID-19.* Retrieved April 21, 2020, from www.aahli.com

NEOM. (2021). *The Line : A Revolution in Urban Living.* www.neom.com

Ramady, M. (2016). *The political economy of WASTA: Use and Abuse of social capital networking.* New York: Springer.

Ramady, M. (2014). *Political, economic and financial country risk analysis of the gulf cooperation council.* New York: Springer.

References

Ramady, M. A. (2010). *The saudi arabian economy: Policies, achievements and challenges.* New York: Springer International.

Ramady, M., & Saee, J. (2007). Foreign Direct Investment: A strategic move for a sustainable free enterprise and economic reform in Saudi Arabia. *Thunderbird International Business Review, 49*(1), 37–56.

Rashad, M. (2021). *Saudi Arabia announces judicial reforms in a move towards codified Law.* February 08, 2021. Reuters. www.reuters.com

Reuters. (2020a). *Oman Income Tax expected in 2022 in fiscal shake up.* Retrieved November 2, 2020.

Reuters. (2020b). G20 agrees on new framework for future debt restructuring. *Argaam*, Retrieved November 13, 2020, from www.reuters.com

Saba, Y. (2020). Saudi Aramco gets $8 billion with jumbo five-part bond deal. *Reuters*, Retrieved November 17, 2020.

Saee, J. (2005). *Managing organizations in a global economy.* Mason, OH: South Western Thomson Learning.

Said, R. (2018). A Monetary Union for the GCC. *Journal of Economics and Development Studies., 6*(4), 67–76.

SAMA. (2020). *King's approval for the Saudi Central Bank Law and change of name of the Saudi Arabian Monetary Authority.* Retrieved November 24, 2020, from www.sama.gov.sa

Saudi Aramco. (2020). *World's first blue ammonia shipment opens new route to a sustainable future.* Retrieved November 13, 2020, from www.saudiaramco.com

Saudi Gazette. (2020). *KSA makes giant leaps towards ditital transformation, covering key sectors, ranks second globally in corproate cybersecurity.* Retrieved November 17, 2020, from www.saudigazette.com

Saudi Press Agency. (2020). *Shoura convened, formed specialized committees, endorsed Central Bank Law.* Retrieved November 16, 2020, from www.spa.gov.sa

Shebab, B. (2016). Perspectives on the GCC monetary union. *Applied Economics and Finance, 3*(1), 54–63.

Wintour, P. (2021). *Arab States agree to end three year boycott of Qatar.* January 05, 2021. The Guardian. www.theguardian.com

World Bank. (2020). *World development indicators.* Washington, DC: World Bank.

Index

A
Ahmad Hamad Al Gosaibi & Brothers (AHAB), 4
Al Rajhi Banking and Investment Corporation in 1988, 23
Anti-money laundering regulations, 6
Arab Monetary Fund (AMF), 74
Aramco, 64, 76, 80, 81
Authority, 24

B
Bankers Security Deposit Accounts (BSDA's), 38
Bank for International Settlements (BIS), 68
Banking Control Law in 1966, 2
Bank supervision, 3
Basle Committee on banking supervision, 22
Blue ammonia, 76
Board of Directors of Saudi Commercial Banks, 22
Business continuity, 6

C
Capital and reserves, 28
Capital Market Authority (CMA), 10, 18, 26, 44, 47, 67, 77
Capital markets, 3
Central Bank, 3, 77
Circular carbon economy, 75
Closed loop system, 75
Cloud Technology, 4

Council of Co-operative Health Insurance (CCHI), 18
Council of Economic and Development Affairs, 66
COVID-19, 23, 27, 37, 39
 analysis, 77
 business model, 60
 challenges, 79
 digital, 77
 digital space, 61
 domestic issuance program, 60
 economic damage, 59
 financial innovation, 79
 financial instruments, 77
 financial sector, 77
 FinTech, 77
 FinTech applications, 79
 FinTech competition, 60
 global economic crisis, 81
 infrastructure, 81
 international markets, 80
 investment banking, 77
 multi-faceted financial sector, 78
 NCB, 60
 OPEC+ members, 79
 private sector, 60
 SAMA measures, 60
 Saudi financial sector, 78
 sectors, 59
 stability, 80
Cradle-to-grave valuation, 75
Crown Prince, 66
Customer deposit growth, 27
Cyber-security threats, 6

D
Debt, 37–40
Debt Management Office (DMO), 38
Debt service to income ratios, 11
Deferred Payment Program, 60
Deputy Governor for Investments, 13
Digital Infrastructure Index, 66
Dynamic countercyclical loan loss provisions, 11

E
E-Commerce Service Fee Support Program, 60
Economic cycles, 12
Electronic Securities Information System (ESIS), 44
Enforcement Law, 55
Engagement groups, 72, 73
Exchange Traded Funds (ETF's), 45

F
Finance Companies Control Law, 55
Finance Lease Law, 55
Finance leasing, 3
Finance track, 72
Financial legal framework, 55, 56
Financial markets, 24
Financial sector, 66
Financial Sector Development Plan/Program (FSDP), 6, 16, 47, 48, 66
Financial Stability Board (FSB), 73
Financial system, 74
Financing, 30, 31, 33
FinTech, 16, 17
Fintech application, 3
Fintech innovation, 6
First Annual Report of 1960, 22
Fixed and floating exchange rate regimes, 11
Fixed peg, 4, 11, 12, 14
Food and Agriculture Organization (FAO), 73
Foreign banks, 22
Foreign Direct Investment (FDI), 62
    domestic and international technology, 61
    economic development, 61
    economy, 63
    investment principles, 64
    investor support, 64, 65
    negative factors, 61
    policies, 64
    positive factors, 61
    SAGIA, 62
    Saudi Arabian Foreign Investment Law, 62
    Saudi FDI program, 64
    Vision 2030 program, 61
FTSE Emerging market, 47

G
General Authority for Small and Medium Enterprises, 30
Global financial crisis, 3
Government bonds, 28
Gross Written Premiums (GWP), 19
G20 Leadership, 70–76
Gulf Cooperation Council (GCC), 68–70
Gulf International Bank, 60

I
Information security, 6
Institution, 1
Insurance sector, 3, 17, 19
International Financial Architecture, 74
International Labor Organization (ILO), 73
International Monetary Fund (IMF), 74
International Organization of Securities Commission, 68
Investment funds, 50
Investment Funds Regulations, 50
Investment process organization chart, 14
Investment segments, 14
Investor support, 64, 65
Islamic Development Bank (IsDB), 74
Islamic Law, 2

K
Kafalah, 60
Kuwait Central Bank, 4

L
"Learning by doing", 2
Liberalization, 22
Liquidity Coverage Ratio (LCR), 11
Liquidity segments, 14
Loan Guarantee Program, 60
Loan to value (LTV), 56
    LTV Ratio, 11

M
Marginal propensity to consume multiplier (MPC), 40
Market capitalization, 22
Market conditions, 12

Index

Ministry of Commerce and Investment (MOCI), 18
Ministry of Finance, 10, 38, 56, 67
Ministry of Investments, 64
Monetary Agency, 22
Monetary policy framework, 7
Mortgage, 53–56
MSCI Emerging market, 47

N
National Bank of Kuwait, 4
National Debt Management Office, 60
National Transformation Program, 53
Netherlands Trading Company, 2
NOMU Parallel Market, 52
Non-performing loans (NPL's), 11

O
Oil price, 64, 79–81
Organization for Economic Cooperation and Development (OECD), 74
Over the Counter (OTC), 46

P
Paris Climate Agreement, 75
POS, 60
Public funds, 50
Public Investment Fund (PIF), 13–16, 24, 35–37, 77
Public Prosecution Office, 74

Q
Qatar, 35, 68, 70
Qualified Foreign Investors (QFI's), 44
Qualified Investors, 52

R
Real Estate Development Fund (REDF), 56
Real Estate Finance Law, 55
Real Estate Investment Traded Funds (REIT's), 45, 53
Recycle, 75, 76
Reduce, 75
Registered Real Estate Mortgage Law, 55
Remove, 76
Reuse, 75
Risk management, 3
Riyad Bank, 26

S
SAMA's evolution
 challenges, 3–6
 economic shock scenarios, 10
 financial institutions, 9
 financial system, 9
 FinTech, 16, 17
 foreign exchange markets, 8
 global financial crisis, 8
 governors, 3–6
 infancy, 1–3
 insurance sector, 17, 19
 macro prudential dashboard, 9
 macro-prudential framework, 7
 macroprudential policy, 9
 macro prudential toolkit, 10, 11
 monetary policy framework, 7
 monetary policy instruments, 8
 national economy, 7
 new banking technology, 16, 17
 pegged currency regime, 11–13
 PIF, 13–16
 public funds, 8
 risk assessment toolkit, 10
Saudi Arabian Foreign Investment Law, 62
Saudi Arabian General Investment Authority (SAGIA), 18, 62
Saudi banking sector, 10
 chaotic financial conditions, 21
 control structure, 21
 effective risk management, 21
 evolution, 22–24, 26
 financing, 30, 31, 33
 growing role, 35–37
 implications, 37–40
 market discipline, 22
 performance, 27–29
Saudi banking system, 4
Saudi banks, 30
Saudi Basic Industries (SABIC), 81
Saudi British Bank, 26
Saudi Capital Market
 financial legal framework, 55, 56
 growth, 53–55
 mobilizing local and foreign investment, 47–51
 NOMU Parallel Market, 52
 Tadawul stock exchange, 44–47
Saudi Central Bank, 4, 77, 79
Saudi Commercial Banks, 27, 29, 40
Saudi Company for Share Registration, 44
Saudi economy, 3
Saudi FinTech Initiative in Cooperation, 16
Saudi Hollandi Bank, 2, 24

Saudi Industrial Development Fund (SIDF), 30, 63
Saudi insurance market, 17
Saudi International Bank (SIB), 4
Saudi leading organizations, 73
Saudi Market Capitalization, 45
Saudi Real Estate Refinance Company (SRC), 54
Saudi Riyal, 2, 7, 8, 11–13, 15, 77
Saudi Silver Riyal, 2
Saudization policy, 23
Securities Clearing Center Company, 44, 45
Securities Depository Center Company, 44
Sherpa track, 72
Small and Medium Sized (SME) segment, 27
Sovereign Wealth Fund (SWF), 35
Special Drawing Right (SDR), 11

T
Tadawul stock exchange, 44–47
Treasury Consolidate accounts (TCA), 40
Treasury Single Accounts (TSA), 40

U
United Nations (UN), 74
Universal banking model, 2

U.S.A.'s Financial Crimes Enforcement Network (Fin CEN), 78
U.S. dollar, 11
U.S. Treasury bills, 14

V
Value Added Tax (VAT), 39
Vietnam, 74
Vision 2030 Financial Plan
  Capital Market initiatives, 68
  digital infrastructure, 66
  economy, 66
  financial sector, 66, 68
  firm foundation, 68
  FSDP program, 67
  implementation, 65
Vision 2030 Realization Plan, 49

W
West Texas Intermediate (WTI), 80
World Bank Group (WBG), 74
World Competitiveness Yearbook (WCY), 75
World Health Organization (WHO), 74
World Trade Organization (WTO), 74

Printed in Great Britain
by Amazon